EVERY THIRD THOUGHT

GIOVANNI RABONI

And thence retire me to my Milan, where
Every third thought shall be my grave.

The Tempest

For my son, Brian,
this book of life and love
and transcendent attachment.

—M. P.

CONTENTS

Preface

I met with Giovanni Raboni for the second—and, sadly, the last—time in February 2004 in Milan. We were accompanied by a mutual friend, the novelist and translator Gayle Ridinger, who translated for both of us (though Raboni admired the poetry of John Berryman and was, at the time of our meeting, doing a translation of Eliot's *Murder in the Cathedral* for performance by a local theater group, as a translator from English he was my mirror image, and could no more converse fluently with me in English than I could with him in Italian). Over lunch, he told us, with a mixture of modesty and pride, that he had just heard that he'd been selected for inclusion in Mondadori's Meridiani series of standard authors (modeled, like the Library of America, on the French Bibliothèque de la Pléiade), an honor almost never conferred on a living writer. He gave a little laugh and said that he hoped it wouldn't turn out to be a curse. Nine weeks later, he suffered an arrhythmia; after waking from a coma of more than three weeks' duration, he spent the next several months in hospitals and rehabilitation facilities until he died of a stroke on September 16. He was seventy-two years old.

Where some, perhaps including Raboni himself, might find premonition or prescience, others of us see a self-effacing casual remark made memorable only because of a ghastly coincidence. But, whatever one's suppositions about such matters may be, it is inarguable that, as testified to by the thick volume he didn't live to see, his death deprived us of a serious and prolific poet who was still working at the height of his powers, still adding to the stock of his already considerable achievement. In my opinion, and I am very far from being alone in it, he is a not only a very fine poet, but a major one. "Major poet" is a term we bandy about quite freely, but what exactly do we mean by it? The best and most detailed definition that I know was given, in the introduction to his 1965 anthology *Nineteenth-Century Minor British Poets*, by W. H. Auden, who is in some significant respects—the variety and abundance of his themes and forms, his passionate social concern, his distinction as a love poet—a writer that Raboni strongly resembles. (It will surprise few, if any, that Auden's criteria fit his own work quite neatly—and Eliot went even further in this direction: gathering a small group of lyrics in his *Collected Poems* under the heading "Minor Poems," he made clear how he intended the rest of the volume to be regarded).

After stating that, in his view, to "qualify as major, a poet . . . must satisfy about three and a half of the following five conditions," Auden proceeds to number and list them, beginning with the assertion that a major poet has to "write a lot." To some this may seem an arbitrary expectation, but Auden is no doubt implying that to be truly major (not necessarily the same thing as good), a poet must expend a great deal of energy and attempt to achieve a great deal, which is often a sprawling and restless as well as a prolific enterprise, as opposed to the neat, little, frequently safe achievements of the talented but less driven. Raboni may not approach the massive output of a Wordsworth, Tennyson, or Browning, whose bodies of work Auden seeks to distinguish from the slender, shapely corpus of someone like Housman; over a fifty-year career, however, he amassed what by modern standards is an admirably bulky collection, one that, excluding adaptations, translations, and theatrical works, runs to nearly six hundred pages.

Auden's second criterion, that the poet needs to display "a wide range of subject matter and treatment," is clearly related to the first. In the case of Raboni, from the terse lyrics of his earliest phase (many of them focused on the passion of Christ) to the scores of sonnets written in his fifties and sixties (a trend toward formalism that reversed the movement of so many of his American contemporaries) to the bitter political commentaries alternating with nostalgic reminiscences that characterized his final phase, his work is a rich blend of both constancy and change. Throughout his career, Raboni fulfills Auden's third demand, for "originality of vision and style," by the striking and often quirky angle of insight peculiar to his work, which nonetheless always remains firmly rooted in the real concerns of real people, as shown by his passionate moral, social, and historical engagement, his preoccupation—at times almost an obsession—with illness and death, and his tracing of the delights and fears of a late love.

That Raboni is "a master of verse technique" (Auden's fourth expectation) is demonstrated everywhere by the iambic bedrock that even the freest of his poems rest upon, by his skillful and often subtle deployment of rhyme, and by his rhythmic versatility, as exemplified in abrupt tonal shifts, experiments with varying line lengths and mixtures of colloquial and arcane diction, and the restless enjambment that characterizes so many of the sonnets. "Mortal Canzonettes," written in the early 1980s, is an especially impressive example of Raboni's technical expertise: as the phrasing creates a tone of hushed beauty totally in keeping with the subject, each succeeding stanza is one line shorter than its predecessor, underscoring the emotions of the aging lover contemplating the contraction of his life and hopes toward their inevitable end. Such mastery is expected of any fine poet, and it hardly separates major from minor, but Auden's concluding demand is one that definitively establishes just such a distinction: he argues that major poets, in contrast to their lesser counterparts, go through clear stages of development, enabling readers to tell instantly where any given poem occurs in the course of that poet's career. That Raboni more than fulfills this expectation should, by this point, be amply clear, and is reinforced even by the very appearance of the poems on the page.

I have appended to the text a translation of a talk that Raboni gave in 1982 about one of his best-known poems, "The Wedding," both for its own inherent interest and as a sort of sentimental gesture: it was through my engagement, early in this project, with this complex and original work that I began to sense that I was dealing not merely with a very good poet but with a great one. (I have also included a translation of a long interview that Raboni gave toward the end of his life, in which the poet himself provides much of the biographical information and description of his work that might otherwise have been given here.) Over the last half century there have been many fine Italian poets and several great ones, but for American readers the canon of twentieth-century Italian poetry has remained limited to Montale, Ungaretti, and Quasimodo. It is long past time for that list to be expanded, and I for one can think of no worthier addition to it than Giovanni Raboni.

MICHAEL PALMA

Introduction

Thus in the darkness now and then a face
is stained with blood, a hand beseeches us—
thus there is someone who
disregards or else one who has in his heart
the communion of the living and the dead.

How many times we have read and heard: the language of Raboni is a plain language, which draws on everyday speech and preserves all the natural prosody of everyday speech. "A staunch partisan of moral and stylistic understatement, he doesn't raise the volume but essentially softens it in order to conceal," Mengaldo wrote in 1978.[1] Is this really the case? Is it really the plain language of a poetry that is as mild and reserved as he was in person, that seems also to possess that natural elegance which he had in person, or is it not, rather, on closer inspection, rugged, inaccessible, filled with precipices, filled with dizzying ascents? Take for example these lines from *Parts of a Requiem* (1957–74):

That you wanted me to be
soft, dirty, helpless
tripping over my own feet,
that I myself go on wanting to be the way
you sweetly crippled
my filial self . . .

Very little seems to be "softened" here, and not even the syntax is plain. Raboni touches a raw nerve, touches just that raw nerve that he flaunts almost indecently, and "gently" takes us to the limits of shamelessness, which makes the mutilation even crueler. We may observe in passing that speech is never used just as it is found, but always undergoes a slight alteration, is always subjected to an imperceptible reworking.

Or take these lines from a love poem of 1965:

The city
shrivels, its rind loses juice and fragrance if I were

just to think of leaving you. There won't be
any place to walk. I'll beat my head against the lampposts.
The blooming of leaves in the avenues a thing
that scrapes inside my throat and makes me vomit.

There's an attitude here that is extremely subjective, not to say frenzied, and, above all, intimate to the point of embarassment.

Finally, to put to rest this so-called stylistic understatement, it's sufficient to cite a sonnet from 1998, whose last two lines seem to be an echo of the last two lines of Pascoli's "The Hour of Barga" (". . . Yes, let us go / back where there are those who love, whom I love so"):

. . . Already a horrible
leprosy's at work, it's devouring the fatuous,

the glittering . . . Ah, let's stay here, let's survive,
papa, mamma! where I love you alive.

Why then, do they talk and go on talking about understatement, attenuation, and a "hidden and indirect discourse," as if about someone who wants to take cover, to hide, to "deal with it from a distance" or "talk about something else"?[2] Because, I believe, he says the violent and terrible things that he says in a manner—his alone—that creates a feeling of tranquility, of mildness; and this feeling is born out of the unerring choice of words, out of the unerring rhythm that is born out of their unerring placement in the line. It is the formal expertise, the metrical-rhythmic wisdom, the stylistic sensibility that engender the calm, the tranquil tone, that make what is rugged seem soft and what is brazen seem reserved. If only there is an appropriate formal effort, or an abundance of a prodigious ear, the result is that the word is made new, calm and ineluctable. And this is the miracle of every great poem. Besides, Raboni always considered the word an instrument of moral responsibility, and formal effort expended over the word confers a literary dignity on the word; he believed, with Walter Benjamin, that "the political value of a literary work is its literary value."

How many times we have read and heard that Raboni belongs to the "Lombard line"[3] of poets: I quote his own words on this subject, given that he is considered one of the best critics of the twentieth century, and given that poet and critic are inseparable, because in him the word "creative" and the word "interpretative" are, indeed, the same instrument of moral responsibility, an inescapable duty toward the "living" and the "real" of which literature is the testimony: "The Lombard tradition, in which I fully recognize myself, is, I believe, something substantially different from what twentieth-century historiography understands as the 'Lombard line'—which I've never understood exactly what that is. I recognize myself—or I hope to be able to recognize myself—in the great Lombard tradition that begins with Illuminism and passes through Manzoni and comes down to Tessa, to Gadda, to Vittorio Sereni, to Clemente Rebora. You see, I believe in this Lombardism in literature, and I feel honored if I can call myself Lombard from this point of view."[4] The features of this Lombardism are "those of ethical commitment on the one hand and a substantial realism on the other."[5] As an example of this Lombardism—indeed, of a "Manzonism" in practice, consider a passage from an autobiographical essay of 1977: "Thanks to the Lazzaretto, to the fact of having been born, so to speak, on its fringes, I believe that I realized in a concrete, physical way—a way that no book, no reading would have provided me—that my city was not only what I saw, houses, streets, squares, living people, but was also full of history—that is, houses, streets, squares that were no longer there and people who were no longer alive, dead people. I realized, in short, that my visible city was filled with invisible history, and that this history was, in turn, filled with pain, with threats, with fear. From that moment, I believe, there came into my poetry the theme of the plague: a metaphorical plague, you understand: plague as contagion and condemnation, as circularity and anonymity of injustice."[6] In Raboni the passion for literature was always a passion for reality and for life, because for him literature is the dignity of man in the world, made up of comprehension of the world and responsibility in the world.

According to Sereni, Raboni looks at death "from the side of the dead";[7] according to Baldacci, there is in Raboni "a way of looking at life from death's point of view."[8] Death is indisputably there, from the start, all along, in his poetry, beginning—as has been repeatedly said—with the reflections on the death of Christ, then proceeding gradually to reflections on the deaths of loved ones and friends, coming at last to those on his own death. But there is nothing lugubrious or agonizing about these reflections ("Death is a part of life, completes it and gives it meaning"[9]): no poet loved life like Raboni (three wives, a tremendous capacity for work, a tremendous quantity of work, and travels, and passions—not only literary: music, art, politics, soccer), and very few can match this splendidly filled life of his.

A poem from the late 1950s ends with these two lines:

> who always manage to find some difference
> between being dead and being alive.

In *Quare Tristis* (1998), a poem ends with these lines:

> thus there is someone who
> disregards or else one who has in his heart
> the communion of the living and the dead.

Raboni considered the idea of the communion of the living and the dead "one of the few pillars" of his "faith—assuming that it is possible to speak of faith"; and he added: "I don't mean to say that I believe that there's a life beyond in which we meet the dead. I believe that the dead are here—that is, I believe that we continue to live with people who are no longer here, that they continue to be a part of our lives." And again: "This idea of the human community as a community made up of the living and the dead is one of the things that are closest to my heart."[10] But what is this "communion," this "community"? It is the sense of history: the sense of all the histories of those who have come before us—even without leaving any trace—, the sense of history as knowledge of human character, and the sense of literature as the history of human character; and compassion for the dead, which recurs continually in his poetry, teaches us compassion for the living. "Pietas"—which comes from "pius," that is, "conscientious, responsible"—means to act according to duty, and, because "our duty is to the rights of others,"[11] it means to act according to justice. This, for Raboni, is the foundation of human society: to feel ourselves united with others, living in the history that we make, for which we are responsible before others who are alive, to render them justice; and to feel ourselves also united with the dead who have come before us and who have made the history in which we live, to render them justice.

Raboni has been called a "civic poet." "I'd like to make clear that, to me, my poems are all political, or else (which is the same thing) none of them are," he said in 1977.[12] "Those poems of mine that someone has called 'civic' are the most 'personal' ones that I've written," he said in 1984.[13] "I believe, on the one hand, that poetry is always civic in some way if it has an ethical foundation," he said in 2003.[14] Perhaps this is the lowest common denominator of the three elements summarily examined here: formal effort, Lombardism, and compassion for the dead, as well as civic commitment, are all premised on this ethical foundation. Those verses of his unerring in sound and rhythm, those "unpredictable and irrefutable"[15] words of his can convey to us a calm joy and a profound pleasure, because the light of a literary and moral wisdom has been dropped into the darkness of torment and of history—his personal history and the history of the entire human race.

PATRIZIA VALDUGA

NOTES

1. Pier Vincenzo Mengaldo, *Poeti italiani del Novecento*, Mondadori 1978.
2. Piergiorgio Bellocchio, "L'itinerario poetico di Raboni," *Quaderni piacentini*, XIV, 57, Nov. 1974–Jan. 1975.
3. Luciano Anceschi, *Linea lombarda: Sei poeti*, Editrice Magenta 1952.
4. *Testimoni del tempo: Atti degli incontri di Piacenza*, Edizioni Vicolo del Pavone, Piacenza, 2003, conference of Jan. 24, 2003.
5. Ibid.
6. *L'approdo letterario*, XXII, n. 77–78, June 1977.
7. Vittorio Sereni, "A partire dal vissuto," preface to *Il più freddo anno di grazia*, S. Marco dei Giustiniani, 1978.
8. Luigi Baldacci, cover flap of *Quare tristis*, Mondadori 1998.
9. *Il futuro della memoria*, video by Egidio Bertazzoni, 1999, transcription by Rodolfo Zucco.
10. Ibid.
11. *Sette*, Nov. 1993.
12. *L'approdo letterario*, cit.
13. Interview by Renato Minore, "Al riparo della paura," *Il Messaggero*, Nov. 8, 1984.
14. *Testimoni del tempo*, cit.
15. "Parole, ritmi e immagini per costruire mondi," *Corriere della Sera*, Feb. 3, 2004.

EVERY THIRD THOUGHT

Selected Poems 1950–2004

GESTA ROMANORUM (1951–1954)

GESTA ROMANORUM (1951–1954)

Il rimorso di san Giovanni Battista

Silenzio. Udite. Io annuncio la sua morte
perché sono di fronte a voi l'autore
della sua venuta e dei suoi giorni
disastrosi. Oh fossi morto prima,
nel deserto, come muoiono i cammelli
che si fidano troppo del proprio gozzo! io così
della mia memoria, della memoria
che Dio mi concede sulle cose future.
Io non volevo ucciderlo
ma la mia fede si è tramutata in pietra o coltello, il mio battesimo
in violento scorpione. Mi perdoni
se troppo poco ho peccato! Io fiorisco di colpa
come la Vergine è fiorita di lui
nel grembo involontario.

The Remorse of Saint John the Baptist

Silence. Hearken. I announce his death
for I am here before you the author of
his coming and of his disastrous days.
Oh, if I had died first, out in
the wilderness, as camels die who put
too much faith in their own gullets! just as I
in my memory, the memory that God
gives me of things that haven't yet occurred.
I didn't want to kill him,
but my faith was changed to a rock or knife, my baptism
into a raging scorpion. Forgive me
if I have sinned too little! I bloom with guilt
just as the Virgin bloomed with him
in her involuntary womb.

Timori della Maddalena

Ho paura del legno e della rupe,
ho paura del corpo, del nervo lacerato,
dei tendini recisi, ho paura della luce,
ho paura del sasso che chiuderà la tua porta,
ho paura del vento e delle voci, ho paura
del corvo che ti mangerà, ho paura del lupo
che troverà le tue ossa, ho paura
che tu sia morto e tutte le notti
avrò paura che tu mi baci di gelo
e mi tiri i piedi sotto il lenzuolo.

Magdalene's Fears

I'm afraid of the wood and rock, I'm afraid
of the body, of the lacerated nerve,
of the slashed tendons, I'm afraid of the light,
I'm afraid of the stone that will block your entranceway,
I'm afraid of the wind and the voices, I'm afraid
of the raven who'll eat you, I'm afraid of the wolf
who's going to find your bones, I am afraid
that you are dead and every night I'll be
afraid you are kissing me with icy lips
and pulling at my feet under the sheet.

Meditazione nell'orto

Ricòrdati: chiudere il gas, le sei mandate alla porta.
C'è rischio di spezzare il calice e c'è rischio di smarrirlo
prima che tutto si compia.
E l'orto non ancora invaso, l'orecchio ancora saldo,
quanti fili dispersi da annodare
perché tutto si compia!
Scegliere chiodi giusti, scegliere il fiele e la spugna,
far le prove con Anna e con Pilato,
discutere la piaga coi lanciatori di coltelli
perché tutto si compia.

Meditation in the Garden

Remember: turn off the gas, six turns of the key in the lock.
There's a risk of breaking the cup and there's a risk of losing it
before all may be fulfilled.
And the garden not yet invaded, the ear still attached,
so many scattered threads to be tied together
so that all may be fulfilled!
To choose the right nails, to choose the gall and the sponge,
to rehearse the trials with Annas and with Pilate,
to discuss the wound with the ones who throw the knives
so that all may be fulfilled.

Orazione di Giuda

O giudei bianchi e neri, compagni
della mia vita in questo fuoco e vento,

ecco, io vi tendo la mano del perdono:
io, l'agnello sacrificante e sacrificato

due volte, nell'amore e nell'odio,
apostolo una volta dell'ulivo

fraterno, una volta dell'ulivo
suicida. E a voi romani tendo la mano

del perdono, perché ogni cosa sia fatta
due volte, e ogni uomo guardi con quattro occhi.

Judas's Oration

O Judeans white and black, companions
of my life within this fire and this wind,

behold, I extend to you the hand of forgiveness:
I, the lamb sacrificing and sacrificed

twice, in love and in hatred, the apostle
once of the fraternal olive tree,

once of the suicidal olive tree.
And to you Romans I extend the hand

of forgiveness, so that everything may be done
twice, and each man look about him with four eyes.

Tradimento di Pietro

Quante volte, pellegrini
affranti da una notte di bufera,
mettendoci alla fine accanto al fuoco
d'una locanda, ci troviamo in mezzo
ai volti stanchi dei nostri nemici!
Certo, potremmo
alzarci urlando; e forse, addirittura
tirar fuori il coltello: e interrogati
sul nostro nome
rispondere coi motti più roventi
fracassando stoviglie. Ma a chi giova
tanta fatica? All'oste no, né al cuore
spossato dalla pioggia. Meglio fingerci amici,
stranieri, o troppo vili: distesi sulla panca
che scivola nell'ombra dai bagliori
rispondere coi cenni o a monosillabi
tirandoci il mantello fin sopra gli occhi.

Peter's Betrayal

How many times, pilgrims
done in by a night of stormy weather,
when we've finally settled down before the fire
at an inn, we find ourselves surrounded by
the weary faces of our enemies!
Sure, we could leap
shouting to our feet, and maybe even
pull out a knife: and if asked for our name
answer with scorching
wisecracks while we start in smashing up
the crockery. But who would profit from
such carrying on? Not the host, and not the heart
drained by the rain. Better pretend to be friends,
strangers, or too craven: stretched on a bench
that's slipping from the fireglow into shadow
answer with nods or monosyllables
pulling the hood of our cloak over our eyes.

Aria per tenore

Crocifiggilo
poiché questo è il mandato
e la stanca vecchiaia s'avvicina.
Inchiodalo nel passo dell'alfiere,
del suonatore di viola, dell'amico
troppo svelto coi dadi.
E ogni volta, a palazzo o nel recinto
del mercato,
dimentica i tuoi sogni e vibra forte,
rapido, fino all'elsa. Crocifiggilo.

Aria for Tenor

Crucify him
because this is the mandate
and weary old age is drawing near.
Nail him to the pace of the standard-bearer,
the viola player, the friend who is
too quick with the dice.
And each time, at the palace or in the enclosure
of the marketplace,
forget about your dreams and deliver hard,
fast, and all the way to the hilt. Crucify him.

Il Centurione

Non bisogna aver fretta di sapere
se uno è buono o cattivo:
c'è tempo per capirlo, e poco tempo
per mettere a profitto la notizia.
Ma se quel dubbio vi tortura, allora
date una mano a suoi persecutori,
fate cuore al carnefice.
Per sciogliere un enigma così strano
la morte è lo strumento più sicuro.

Ne ho visti tanti morire! Un malfattore
non muore così, ma gridando di paura
come un bambino; o spavaldo, con la faccia da eroe
e modi bruschi. Disperato e insieme
sereno, così forte a pazientare,
so che muore soltanto un innocente.

The Centurion

No need to hurry when you want to know
if someone's good or evil:
there's time to piece it out, and not much time
to put the information to good use.
But if you're still tormented by that doubt,
then lend a helping hand to his persecutors,
give heart to his executioner.
For solving so peculiar an enigma
death is the most reliable instrument.

I've watched so many die! A criminal
doesn't die like this; instead, he wails in terror
like a baby, or else insolent, with the face of a hero
and rough manners. Hopeless and yet
serene, so strong in bearing up patiently,
I know that only an innocent man dies.

Alba

Ormai fa giorno. Non basta
sedere gravemente sulla sedia di paglia
vestito di canna e di sangue
ascoltando le ingiurie dei soldati, ospitando nel fianco
l'orma sintetica della lancia. Perché sia giorno bisogna
avere gli occhi lontani dalla guancia,
l'unghia sparsa dal dito,
una mano di calce sopra il cuore.

Dawn

It's already day. It's not enough
to sit there gravely on a wicker seat
dressed in cane and blood
listening to the soldiers' insults, housing the concise
mark of the spear in your side. For it to be day you need
to have your eyes far from your cheek,
nails loosened from your fingers,
a coat of lime over your heart.

Partita

Il gioco della civetta nella camera buia,
il duello rischiarato da un'unica candela
non reggono il confronto con la partita d'offese
tra un uomo legato e i suoi vigili custodi.
Tutto pieno di lividi e confuso
il poverino aguzzerà l'ingegno
per sciogliere una almeno delle nostre sciarade
e rimediare alla brutta figura.
Quanti spiriti sottili in un corpo di guardia!
Una sorte propizia ci ha riuniti.
In così buona compagnia ciascuno
sente il valore dei propri bons mots.

Round

The game of owl played in a dark room,
the duel fought by the light of a single candle
don't measure up against a round of insults
between a bound man and his keen-eyed keepers.
Covered all over with bruises and confused
the wretched fellow has to hone his wits
to solve at least one of our charades and cut
a better figure for himself.
How many *esprits* in just one *corps* of guardsmen!
Propitious fate has brought us back together.
And in such splendid company each one
senses the value of his own *bons mots*.

Epigramma

Ha fede nei discepoli? Per ora,
mentre delusi perdono la testa
e accorciano le orecchie ai servitori,
è lui la pietra e Pietro la balestra.

Epigram

Does he have any faith in his disciples?
For now they're all frustrated, with the result
they lose their heads and lop the ears off people,
and he's the rock and Peter the catapult.

Personaggio di sfondo di una crocifissione

Un po' avanti negli anni
non è l'amore, è il gioco che fa complici
e promuove gli accordi. È qui che cerco
gli amici — e qui li trovo: battitori,
raccattapalle.
Questo è il mio posto ormai: non fra i miei pari
ma fra i vili e gli sguatteri, fioriti
intorno a me per chiudere le porte
che dimentico aperte, per finire
la quaglia che ho ferito,
per dare un'ultima volta le carte
se mi trema la mano o il cuore è stanco.

Figure in the Background of a Crucifixion

Getting on a bit in years
it isn't love, it's pastimes that create
accomplices and promote arrangements. It's here
I look for friends—and here I find them: beaters,
ballboys.
This is my place from now on: not among my peers
but among the low and the scullery boys, who bloom
around me on all sides to close the doors
that I forget to shut, to finish off
the quail I wounded,
to deal out one last hand of cards
if my hands tremble or my heart is tired.

Coro

Da quante bugie ci libera la morte
di un amico! L'angoscia, il batticuore
che una menzogna gli sia rivelata
ridiventano nulla in un istante.
E dietro il suo sguardo che lentamente s'inclina
al pavimento della stanza o s'incanta nel buio
il nostro cuore risorge così semplice, fiero
dei nostri falsi antenati e delle oziose abitudini.

Chorus

How many lies we're liberated from
when a friend dies! The anguish, the apprehension
that some falsehood will find its way to him
all suddenly set at nothing once again.
And behind his gaze that slowly slips away
down to the floor or stays fixed in the darkness,
our hearts rise up so simple and so proud
of our phony forebears and our lazy ways.

Altre interviste

Il falegname

Chi cerca
trova. Per risparmiare del legno
invece di inchiodarlo su un quadrato,
su un triangolo isoscele, su un cerchio,
si può metterlo in croce.

La lavandaia

Ho cercato del sangue
in questa faccia livida, rappresa
sul pannolino.
Ho battuto la treccia del bucato
sulla solita pietra
per cancellare i disegni del pus.
Ho raccolto la cesta. Mi son messa,
lottando ancora, per via.

Il chirurgo

C'è colpo e colpo. Ci sono ferite di striscio
che nessuno può guarire
e uomini che muoiono a ottant'anni
di coltellate prese in gioventù.
Non c'è regola. Qualcuno si salva

The Carpenter

Seek
and ye shall find. In order to save wood
instead of nailing him up on a square,
on an isosceles triangle, on a circle,
we can put him on a cross.

The Washerwoman

I looked for the blood
in this livid face, clotted
on the linen cloth.
I pounded the twisted laundry
on the usual rock
to wash away the patterns of the pus.
I gathered up the hamper. I set out,
still struggling, on my way.

The Surgeon

There are blows and there are blows. There are little nicks
that nobody can heal
and men who die at eighty years of age
from stab wounds that they got when they were young.
There isn't any rule. Somebody's saved

e si fa prete. A qualcuno la vista
s'indebolisce. A volte
i coltelli rispuntano dal cuore
nel senso della lama.

Il fornaio

Non chiederò
consigli a destra e sinistra.
So cosa devo fare.
Non lievito. Quantità di farina.
Una mattina all'alba m'alzerò
come sempre, come ora.
È solo una questione di spessore.
Vivo sarò
questa spada dei morti
guardando l'acqua, la cenere,
la boria dei garzoni.

and turns priest. Somebody else's eyesight
fades away. Sometimes
the knives come sticking up out of the heart
blade first.

The Baker

I won't ask
for advice left and right.
I know what I have to do.
Not leaven. A measure of flour.
One morning at the dawn hour I'll rise
like always, like now.
It's only a question of thickness.
Living I'll be
this sword of the dead
watching the water, the ashes,
the swagger of the shop-boys.

A Tarbes

A Tarbes cantando fanti e regine, riversi
su davanzali di pietra e broccato, aridamente divisi
in rettangoli di regno con larghi margini, una sera
vennero a lungo con me, picche e picche, quadri e quadri,
finché tornai al mio albergo in una strada di mendicanti.

At Tarbes

At Tarbes singing jacks and queens, turned over
on windowsills of stone and brocade, drily divided
into large-margined rectangles by realm, came a long way
with me one evening, spades and spades, diamonds and diamonds,
until I got back to my hotel on a street of beggars.

Testimoni

Qui il duca fa pugnalato, e questo è il pozzo
dove si sbarazzarono del corpo
fino all'alba. M'immagino la scena.
Ma fra tante finestre, sottoporteghi, scale
chissà quante parole della rissa
trovarono orecchi avidi e timorati, cuori
pronti a soffrire quest'altro segreto
per carità di patria. O a bisbigliarlo
più tardi, in fin di vita, nell'orecchio peloso
del confessore. Circolazione di notizie
nel buio delle viscere.

Witnesses

Here is where they stabbed the duke, and this
is the well where they rid themselves of the body
until the dawn arrived. I imagine the scene.
But with so many windows, tunnels, stairs
who knows how many words of the struggle found
greedy and scrupulous ears, and hearts that were
ready to endure this other secret
for love of country. Or to whisper it
much later, at death's door, in the hairy ear
of the father confessor. Circulation of news
in the darkness of the guts.

Dal crepuscolo all'alba

Chiudi in fretta lo splendido messale e parla
con la forma più stanca dell'Agnello,
con i lividi segni che la pioggia può lavare
prima della campana, molto prima dell'alba,
prima che il coltello si sfili dal costato
e voli luccicando verso il forno operoso.

From Twilight to Dawn

Close the splendid missal hastily
and speak with the wearier figure of the Lamb,
with the livid signs the rain can wash away
before the bell rings, long before the dawn,
before the knife is unsheathed from his side
and flies glistening toward the busy oven.

Requiem per compleanno

Lo sai com'è gennaio qui da noi: ricordi
che certe volte ogni cosa diventa
più stretta d'un grumo di terra, d'una pietra,
più stretta d'una croce. Così, credo,
non serve che ti dica di pregare
per i morti. Nessuno più di loro
è preso senza scampo in questa trappola
di corda grossa e corteccia
che le mani gelate non riescono a slegare.

Requiem for a Birthday

You know what January's like here: you recall
how there are times when everything becomes
narrower than a clot of earth, a stone,
narrower than a cross. So, I believe,
there isn't any point in telling you
to say prayers for the dead. No one is caught
more than they are with no escape inside
this trap made out of tree bark and thick ropes
that frozen hands can't manage to undo.

Congedo

Le parole scambiate col barbiere
sapendole aride e vane, credendole fraintese
e sepolte per sempre in un orecchio peloso
ritornano. Più fioche, più crudeli
girano senza sosta nei miei sogni,
turbano il mio riposo. Non m'è dato correggerle, ormai,
né scacciarle dall'umida bottega.

Envoi

The words exchanged with the barber,
knowing them arid and hollow, thinking them misunderstood
and buried forever in a hairy ear
come back. Fainter, crueler than before
they whirl around unendingly in my dreams,
they trouble my repose. By now I have no power to correct them,
or to sweep them out of the damp shop.

da LE CASE DELLA VETRA (1955–1965)

from THE HOUSES OF THE VETRA (1955–1965)

1955–1959

1955–1959

Tovaglia

A che serve parlare con gli amici?
quasi tutti s'arrabbiano, o ridendo
si picchiano la fronte. Si parla di dissesti,
di cantanti invecchiate o dimagrite. Fuori
la notte si gonfia come un gufo.
E siamo pochi, troppo pochi a patire
tanti capi d'accusa:
l'uovo, il pane, il bicchiere
posati sulla mensa
come parchi strumenti di tortura.

Tablecloth

What use is there in talking to our friends?
almost all of them get mad, or smack their brows,
laughing. They talk about financial problems,
of singers who've grown old or thin. Outside
the night is puffed up like an owl.
And we are few, too few to endure so many
counts of indictment:
the egg, the bread, the glass
set out on the table
just like frugal instruments of torture.

Ponzio P.

Al fondo
d'un orrido paese che non ha inverno, rettore
di teste calde, giudice di liti
senza capo né coda
— cos'altro può volere il più maligno
dei padri? Solo in sogno mi riporta
al verde inciso dei prati, ai piaceri d'un tempo
che non ritorna: il trotto nel maneggio
deserto,
le delicate azioni campestri,
le giubbe rosse per strangolare la volpe
dietro l'utima siepe.
                                        Realtà
è lo squallore dei viaggi, la carriera mal digerita,
le raccomandazioni che non servono a niente
o arrivano in ritardo; è avere, invece
dello stagno grigio e mattutino, pieno
di pigra cacciagione,
questo sporco catino dove mi lavo le mani.

Pontius P.

In the depth
of a wretched country with no winter, governor
of hotheads, arbiter of squabbles
with neither head nor tail
—what more than this could the most malign of fathers
wish for? Only in dreams does he bring me back
to the etched green of meadows, to the pleasures of a time
that doesn't return: the trot of a wilderness
horseback ride,
the delicate rustic motions,
the scarlet jackets for strangling the fox
behind the last hedgerow.
                                        Reality
is the dreariness of journeys, the hard to stomach career,
the recommendations that aren't worth a damn
or that arrive too late; it's having, instead
of the gray early-morning pond, full
of lazy game,
this filthy basin where I wash my hands.

Una volta

Di gente ricca solo
coi bachi e le filande credo
non ci sia più nessuno: ma una volta
nel Comasco o a Bergamo, da dove
viene la mia famiglia,
molte fortune si contavano a gelsi
e con quante ragazze venivano a filare
i bozzoli scottati per ammazzare le farfalle
nelle fredde officine. Se penso
a chi è la gente ricca adesso, a cosa
gli costa il capitale,
mi convinco che tutto si complica, anche il male.
Una volta le colpe dei padroni
erano così semplici! Il padrone
d'oggi, consiglio d'amministrazione
o gruppo di maggioranza, è un peccatore
un po' troppo sui generis per me . . .

Once

Of those who got rich
solely from caterpillars and spinning mills,
I doubt there are any left these days: but once
in the towns around Como or in Bergamo,
where my family is from,
plenty of fortunes were reckoned in mulberry trees
and by how many young girls came to spin
cocoons that were scalded to kill the butterflies
in the chilly factories. If I think about
who the rich are nowadays, about what
their capital costs,
I'm convinced that everything's complicated, even evil.
Once the bosses' crimes
were so simple! The boss of modern times,
a board of directors or a group
of majority shareholders, is a sinner
a little too *sui generis* for me . . .

Risanamento

Di tutto questo
non c'è più niente (o forse qualcosa
s'indovina, c'è ancora qualche strada
acciottolata a mezzo, un'osteria).
Qui, diceva mio padre, conveniva
venirci col coltello . . . Eh sì, il Naviglio
è a due passi, la nebbia era più forte
prima che lo coprissero . . . Ma quello
che hanno fatto, distruggere le case,
distruggere quartieri, qui e altrove,
a cosa serve? Il male non era
lì dentro, nelle scale, nei cortili,
nei ballatoi, lì semmai c'era umido
da prendersi un malanno. Se mio padre
fosse vivo, chiederei anche a lui: ti sembra
che serva? è il modo? A me sembra che il male
non è mai nelle cose, gli direi.

Renewal

Of all this
there's nothing left anymore (or maybe something
that you can still make out, there's still a street
or two half-paved with cobblestones, a tavern).
Down here, my father said, you were well advised
to carry a knife with you . . . Ah yes, the Canal
is just a few steps away, the fog was stronger
back then, before they covered it . . . But what
they've gone and done, destroying all the houses,
destroying neighborhoods, here and other places,
what good is it? The sickness wasn't there
inside them, in the stairways, in the courtyards,
in the galleries, if anything it was
the damp that could make you sick. If my father were
alive today, I would ask him: Does it seem
good to you? Is this the way? It seems to me
that the sickness is never in things, I'd say to him.

Rammarico del viceré

Non si va avanti né indietro.
Non si guarda né a destra né a sinistra,
né in basso né in alto. Tutto, ormai,
filerebbe secondo le istruzioni
se non fosse per questi apostoli di merda,
per queste incredibili dodici persone
che fra essere morti e essere vivi
trovano sempre qualche differenza.

The Viceroy's Regret

There's no going forward or going back.
There's no looking either right or left,
either high or low. Everything, by now,
would have gone according to instructions
if only it hadn't been for those shitty apostles,
for those twelve unbelievable characters
who always manage to find some difference
between being dead and being alive.

19**

Certo, è il momento di parlare
come c'è stato quello di tacere
con tutti (perfino con gli amici), attenti
a non far mai la stessa strada,
e non lasciare in giro taccuini
stracciati, indirizzi di streghe. E il tempo aiuta,
eh? non è vero? (Anche troppo.) Ma se uno
è appena astuto, sa che non bisogna
lasciarsi andare. E così, niente abbracci
al baritono negro, allo scienziato
ebreo per parte di madre, niente fiori
sulle fosse o rimproveri sgarbati
agli aguzzini. Quando più te l'aspetti
torna a tirare un'aria di cappucci.

19**

Yes, certainly, there is a time to speak
just as there was a time for keeping quiet
with everybody (even with friends), and being
careful never to take the same road twice,
or to leave torn notebooks lying around,
or the addresses of witches. And time helps,
right? Doesn't it? (Even too much.) But anyone
the least bit savvy knows that there's no need
to go to hell with oneself. So, no embraces
for the Negro baritone, for the scientist
who's Jewish on his mother's side, no flowers
on graves and no impolitic reproaches
to torturers. Just when you most expect it
comes a hint of hooded figures in the air.

Cinema di pomeriggio

Quasi sempre, a quest'ora
arriva gente un po' speciale (però
di buonissimo aspetto). Chi si siede
ma poi continua a cambiar posto,
chi sta in piedi, sul fondo della sala, e fiuta,
fiuta rari passaggi, la bambina
mezzo scema, la dama ch'entra sola,
la ragazza sciancata . . . Li guardo per sapere
che storia è la loro, chi li caccia. Quando
viene la luce penso come il cuore
gli si deve contorcere cercando
d'esser salvo più in là, di sprofondare
nel buio che torna tra un minuto.

Movie Theater in the Afternoon

Almost always, at this hour
come people who are a bit peculiar (but
of excellent appearance). One who sits
but keeps on getting up to change his seat,
the one on his feet at the back of the hall who sniffs,
sniffs out unusual passageways, the little
half-witted girl, the lady who comes by herself,
the girl with the bad leg . . . I watch them all
to learn what their stories are, who's hunting them.
When the houselights come back up I think of how
the heart must writhe within as they look to be
safe a bit further on, to sink into
the darkness that returns in just a minute.

Dalla mia finestra

Eh, le misure della notte, l'ambiguo
lume di luna che confonde
il protocollo dei marmi, l'ombra che ravviva
gli strombi delle finestre, le profonde
gole dei cornicioni
scampati (ancora per poco) al viceregno
delle imprese, al morso dei capitali
premiati col sette, sette e mezzo per cento mentre sai, con la
campagna
è già tanto se copri le tue spese . . .

From My Window

Ah, the night's measures, the ambiguous
moonlight that confounds
the protocol of the marbles, the shadow
that revives the jambs of the windows, the deep
grooves of the cornices
preserved (for a little while yet) from the viceregency
of the building firms, from the bite of capital
repaid with seven, seven and a half percent, while you know, out
in the country
it's saying a lot if you cover your expenses . . .

Portale

Difficile dire
quante spade, quante lance, quanti elmi di cuoio
su profili romani,
quanti fabbri e pescatori col cappelluccio a cono
e le orecchie puntute,
quante facce di porco o di drago, quanti piedi
con cinque dita

e ruote e focacce sbilenche e proiezioni
di tavole imbandite

nella ressa, nel fuoco, nella gioia
della neve che approssima, del vino
bevuto in gioventù,
della folla irta e viva, di un'intera nazione
che pesca caccia ecc. e prepara
l'acre festa sul legno.

Portal

Hard to say
how many swords, how many lances, how many leather helmets
on Roman profiles
how many blacksmiths and fishermen with conical caps
and pointed ears
how many pig or dragon faces, how many feet
with five toes

and lopsided wheels and loaves and projection views
of well-stocked tables

in the crowd, in the flame, in the joy
of the snow that's on its way, of the wine
drunk in days of youth,
of the lively bristling crowd, of a whole nation
that fishes hunts etc. and prepares
the acrid feast over wood.

L'errore coloniale

Lo so: ma chi ha il coraggio
di crederli dei porci? Se li penso
uno per uno: il primo, poveraccio
di giardiniere o cuoco, capitato
chissà da dove
a raccontare una storia di streghe
forse sognata, forse inventata, certo
non vera; l'altro a scrivere su fogli
mezzo stracci, con lettere contorte,
una denuncia regolare: uno
che non gli importa niente, che ha
voglia solo di andarsene a dormire
fino a domani; il terzo, poliziotto
con sigaro e bombetta
pronto a prendere a schiaffi gli indiziati
ma anche a portargli dell'acqua da bere
in bicchieri di carta; tutti, fino al
giudice coloniale
dall'astratta parrucca a cannelloni
— ecco, chi avrà il coraggio, guardandoli uno a uno,
di dargli addosso? E poi, come Gide dice
che un ragazzino diceva di Cristo,
il fallait bien qu'on le cloue pour qu'il tienne.

The Colonial Error

I know: but who has the nerve
to consider them pigs? If I think about them
one by one: the first one, a poor devil
of a gardener or a cook, who's come here
from who knows where
telling some kind of story about witches
maybe dreamed, maybe made up, surely
not true: the other one writing on sheets of paper
torn halfway into strips, in twisted letters,
a standard denunciation: one
to whom nothing matters in the least,
who only wants to go to sleep until
tomorrow; and the third, a police detective
with his cigar and derby
who's always ready to slap a suspect around
but just as ready to bring him a drink of water
in a paper cup: all of them, all the way
to the colonial judge
in his abstract peruke of cannelloni
—so then, who'll have the nerve, looking them over one by one,
to take it to them? And besides, just as Gide says
that a little boy once said about Christ,
il fallait bien qu'on le cloue pour qu'il tienne.

I morti e i veri

Nella casa umida, il poco
ch'è asciutto sembra più asciutto ancora:
nelle stanze da letto al primo piano
il pavimento d'assi quasi bianche
non lucidate con la cera e
un po' distanti; sotto, nella sala
del bigliardo, l'avorio dei birilli
messi in croce . . . (Prima o dopo ci torno
a vedere la casa degli amici
dove a momenti ti nasceva un figlio
— è nato due giorni dopo — e s'aspettava,
di sera, che il temporale portasse
un po' di fresco anche a Milano. Smorti
lungo i muri, con facce da lenoni
o da tartufi, oscuri
antenati lombardi
controllavano il conto delle uova
e dei formaggi: usando astuzia, e quantità
di penne d'oca. Si rideva di loro
con ribrezzo. Ma in fondo, che sia giusto
così? Meglio dei nostri veri, gente
distratta, malinconica
per vizi più sottili, chi può dire
che non sia quello il tipo d'antenati
che nostro figlio fingerà d'avere, ridendo
di loro, voltandogli le spalle
come nessuno è mai riuscito a fare!)

The Dead and the Real

In the humid house, the little bit
that's dry seems even drier than it is:
in the bedrooms on the upper floor
the floorboards practically white
and unwaxed and a little far
apart; downstairs, in the billiard room,
the ivory of the ninepins that have been
laid crosswise . . . (Sooner or later I return
to see the house of friends
where you were about to give birth to a son
—he was born two days later—and we waited,
in the evening, for the storm to bring a bit
of fresh air down to Milan. Along
the walls, pale, with the faces of pimps
or Tartuffes, obscure
Lombard ancestors
who used to tally the accounts of eggs
and cheeses: using cunning, and an abundance
of goose-quill pens. We used to laugh at them
disgustedly. But is that really
fair? Better than our real ones, distracted
people, melancholy
because of subtler vices, who can say
that isn't just the kind of ancestors
our son will pretend to have, laughing at them
and turning his back on them the way
no one has ever really managed to do!)

1960–1961

1960–1961

Romanzo

Ma in casa dell'impiccato se di corda
non si deve parlare
di cosa mai parleremo? questi
erano quella sera del lontano
millenovecentosessanta eccetera salendo
tre gradini di marmo prima dell'ascensore i pensieri
o pressapoco
di un certo giovane uomo del quale però per il momento
non ho tempo né voglia di occuparmi.

Novel

But if it's true you should never mention rope
in the house of the hanged man
then what can we ever talk about? these
were on that evening in distant
nineteensixty etcetera going up
three marble steps in front of the elevator the thoughts
or close enough
of a certain young man about whom all the same for the moment
I have neither the time nor the wish to concern myself.

Una città come questa

non è per viverci, in fondo: piuttosto
si cammina vicino a certi muri,
si passa in certi vicoli (non lontani
dal luogo del supplizio) e parlando
con la voce nel naso
avidi, frettolosi si domanda: non è qui
che buttavano i loro cartocci gli untori?

A City Like This

isn't for living in, after all: instead
you go walking close to certain walls,
you wander through certain passageways (not very
far from where the torture went on) and talking
through your nose
you greedily, hastily ask: isn't it here
that the plague-spreaders used to dump their bags?

Canzone

Quando piove, fanno proprio schifo
le finestre che si coprono d'unto, la stufa
che manda fumo negli angoli e in cucina
il sale che si blocca, la cerata
che appiccica . . . Ma trovarsi bene
o trovarsi male, questa è un'altra cosa.
I bambini che vanno su e giù
per il ballatoio schiantando rami secchi
col fianco, fanno paura, mi sembrano un po' gnomi
dagli occhi: sembra che stiano per volare
sopra il tetto. Ma io dico che da qui
a voler tornare dov'ero, magra
per la fame, mangiata dai pidocchi,
ci corre.

Song

It's so disgusting every time it rains,
the windows covered up with grease, the stove
pouring smoke into the corners and in the kitchen
clumps in the salt, the oilcloth on the table
turning all sticky . . . But whether I'm doing well
or doing badly, that's another matter.
The children who go running up and down
the gallery, their bodies breaking dry branches,
scare me, and when I look at their eyes they make me think
of gnomes: they look like they're about to fly
over the roof. But still, I say, to go back
from here to where I was, a woman worn thin
by hunger, eaten up by lice, well, that's
a different story.

La carriera del bruto

Si fa presto
a chiamare così un poveraccio (sia pure
un povero diavolo, veramente): ma ci pensi
che groviglio, che buio
quante cose difficili da nominare
per una faccia come la sua e un giorno
come questo!
                        Alla fine, si capisce,
è il gesto che decide: se uno
divora una bambina, o tira il collo
a una vecchia stiratrice (inamidava
i colletti a Mussolini, pensa), non c'è rimedio
né per lui né per loro, non c'è Cristo.

The Career of the Brute

How quick we are
to say that some poor creature's one (even when
he's only a poor devil): but think about it,
such confusion and such darkness,
so many things so hard to put a name to
for a face like his and a day
like this!
                In the end, you understand,
the deed decides: if somebody devours
a little baby girl, or wrings the neck
of an old laundress (think of it, she starched
Mussolini's collars), there's no remedy,
not for him and not for them, there is no Christ.

A mio figlio in campagna

Quando va via la luce in campagna
salta fuori tanta gente ch'era sparita
i pezzi del domino coagulano per terra
dal buio della finestra entrano rami
e si dice pazienza, pazienza (bisogna avere
pazienza con la Edison) e senti colpi
scolorire, farsi croste sulle ferite aspettando
la lumaca, la mamma, il bruco,
il grillo parlante con la candela.

To My Son in the Country

When the light dies away out in the country
people who'd disappeared rise up outside
pieces of dominoes coagulate on the ground
branches come in from the darkness of the window
and folks say patience, patience (you have to have
patience with the Edison) and you feel blows
fading, crusts forming on wounds waiting for
the snail, mama, the caterpillar,
the talking cricket with the candle.

Abbastanza posto

Passa il tempo, ci sentiamo
più grandiosi ogni giorno: però
siamo sempre la gente che tira su il sopracciglio
o si gratta la punta del naso, continuiamo
a pensare che tipi così (*quello*
che striscia e non ha palpebre quello che fa
l'amore con le forchette e con la corda) siano,
rispetto a noi, qualcuno — a non capire
che c'è abbastanza posto per ciascuno di loro
in ciascuno di noi.

Room Enough

Time passes, we feel ourselves
growing grander every day: and yet
we're still the people who raise an eyebrow or scratch
the ends of our noses, we go on thinking that those
kinds of people (*that one who creeps*
along and has no eyelids that one who makes love
with forks and with a rope) are, compared to us,
somebody else—to keep from realizing
there's room enough for every one of them
in every one of us.

E tu cosa

E tu invece, gomme di bicicletta
o antenne, cosa credi che sia
questo ronzio che sale dalla nebbia, dai bordi
dell'autostrada, a un tiro di fucile,
sembrerebbe, dal casello di dazio — chi ci aspetta
bel caldo in una tuta di nailon, col muso
nella marcita?

And You, What

And you on the other hand, bicycle tires
or aerials, what do you think it is,
this buzzing that rises from the fog, from the shoulders
of the highway, a rifle shot away,
it would seem, from the tollbooth—who's waiting for us
nice and warm in a nylon jumpsuit, with his mug
in the irrigated meadow?

1962–1965

1962–1965

Il cotto, il vivo

Dopo dieci anni tirarli su. A Musocco
c'è bisogno di posto e il posto si fa
mettendo un morto sopra l'altro, sigillati
in un pezzo di muro. Muovere un campo dopo l'altro. Questo
mese
il campo 49, dov'era sepolto mio padre. Non vorrai
lasciarlo davvero in questo buco
da incubo: corpo coi mattoni: finirà
che non avrai mai voglia di venire
a trovarlo. Ma lascia stare, non andrei
neanche nel cimitero di campagna
che aveva visto da vivo e credo
che gli sarebbe piaciuto. E poi adesso
chi può più dirlo. Adesso che non vuole
più niente, forse son proprio queste cose
che vuole di meno: la fragranza
dell'erba, la povertà della croce,
il nome schiarito dalla pioggia. Forse ama
di più un pezzo di muro, sente
gli spigoli giusti, le opere della malta, mischiarsi
sabbia e calce, connettersi il cotto
e il vivo, gli spigoli, le ossa dei vicini . . .

The Brick, the Stone

Pull them up after ten years. At Musocco
they need the room and they are making room
by putting one body on top of another, sealed
in a piece of a wall. Move one section after another. This month
section 49, where my father was buried. You really
wouldn't want to leave him in this nightmare
pit: body with bricks: in the end it'll be
that you never feel the urge to come
to see him. But forget it, I wouldn't even
have gone to the cemetery in the country
that he saw when he was alive and I believe
he'd have really liked it there. And now
who can say any more? Now that he doesn't
want anything any more, maybe these are
the very things he wants the least: the fragrance
of the grass, the poverty of the cross,
the name clarified by the rain. Maybe
he prefers a piece of wall, he feels
the rightness of the corners, the works of mortar, mixing
sand and lime, connecting the brick
and the stone, the corners, the bones of those around him . . .

Lezioni di economia politica

Cosa vuoi che ti dica. Più tardi
può darsi che la maschera si tagli e tu riesca
a vederli con gli occhi i veri,
i santi moti del tuo cuore . . . tardi
per assecondarli, magari: ma allora,
a diciotto, diciannove anni e nessuno
che ci dicesse sul muso « stronzi », il nostro modo
di rivoltarci era quello, il conformismo,
la pacatezza, il freddo disgusto
per le intemperanze giovanili;
aver schifo della rivoluzione . . .
Uno come lui, capisci, era per forza il nostro uomo
con i suoi colletti rotondi e duri, la spilla,
le scarpe da vampiro. E ti ricordi,
non ne perdevamo una: issati
sui vecchi banchi (dalle porte-finestre il giardino
delle Reali Fanciulle o come diavolo
si chiamavano), immobili, cascando
di sonno, d'incertezza e insieme
impalati d'orgoglio, mi sforzavo
d'essere alla sua altezza, come lui
lucido e spassionato — di capire
com'è giusto applicare anche ai salari, alle teste
degli operai
la legge della domanda e dell'offerta.

Lessons of Political Economy

What do you want me to tell you. Later on
the mask may be cut away and you'll be able
to see with your own eyes the true,
the holy impulses of your heart . . . late
to indulge them, in all likelihood; but then
at eighteen, nineteen years of age and no one
to call us "little shits" right to our faces, that was
the way that we rebelled, conformity,
placidity, a cold disgust
for all the excesses of youth;
a cultivated hatred of revolution . . .
Someone like him, you see, was bound to be
our man, with his hard round collars, his tie-pin,
his bloodsucker shoes. And you remember,
we didn't miss a single one of them: raised
on those old benches (through the French windows
the garden of the Royal Maidens or whatever
the hell they were called), immobile, dropping off
with sleep, with uncertainty, but still
rigid with haughtiness; I strained myself
to measure up to him, to be clearheaded
and dispassionate like him—to understand
how it is just and fair to apply even to wages, to
the heads
of the laborers, the law of supply and demand.

Suicidio in infermeria

In un branco di solidi, trasparenza
di gocce d'acqua. Pelli
d'arancia. Le sponde del lettino. E
la fatica che ha fatto. Assopito
fra due guanciali, fra una morte
che striscia e una che aspetta così
timide, sfuocate nel semicerchio
dell'ombra — scuotersi
da capo, ci pensi?, raggiungere a tastoni
il bianco della lampada, inforcare gli occhiali
per afferrarne un'altra, più vicina, specifica
come il vetro, la plastica, il cartone . . .

Suicide in the Infirmary

In a cluster of solids, the transparency
of drops of water. Orange
peels. The edges of the cot. And
the effort that it took. Drowsing
between two pillows, between one death
that creeps along and one that waits like that,
both timid, blurry in the semicircle
of shadow—rousing himself
once more, can you imagine? groping for
the white of the lamplight, putting on his glasses
to grasp another one, nearer, as specific
as glass, or plastic, or cardboard . . .

Una specie di tic

Quante volte a chi
mi chiedeva notizie di mio padre
ho risposto « non c'è male ». Ma se era
morto da giorni, forse da mesi! Già, è abbastanza
difficile da capire — o forse è come
non sei tu a ricordare: *nascondi*
agli amici un malato, lo senti dietro il muro che arranca
da solo verso il gabinetto
e poteva succedere e hai sventato con le tue
losche preghiere. O forse sarà stato
una specie di tic, accenni di nevrosi . . .

A Sort of a Tic

How many times I've said
to someone who was asking me for news
about my father, "He's not too bad." And he
had been dead for days, maybe even months! Really, it's hard
enough to comprehend—or maybe it's
as if it's not you who recollects: *you hide*
a sick man from your friends, you hear him behind the wall hobbling
toward the toilet by himself
and it might have happened it and you prevented it with
your dubious prayers. Or it may have been
a sort of a tic, suggestions of neurosis . . .

Bambino morto di fatica ecc.

1

La porta chiusa alle spalle, nel buio, d'età
fra cinque e sei anni sopportando
una crescita d'occhi, improvvisamente,
nella schiena e — il plafone ribàltasi in piancito
e qui, e qui, sul pianerottolo (la porta
da dentro chiusa alle spalle) cosa resta da fare
se non cercare scampo con la testa cioè
incastrarla, tra ferro e ferro, sul vuoto delle scale
scabrosamente non riuscendo più a liberarla, minuziosamente
        arrestando
i battiti del cuore
per infarto: tipico dei grandi; questo è uno dei modi.

2

Adesso che me l'hai detto vedo
com'è finito il bambino:
un medio grumo di sangue sul pavimento
del bagno. E tu che se per caso
svenivi, se non c'era nessuno
potevi morire dissanguata. Del quale
comportamento, suggerisci sentimentale,
bisognerebbe ringraziarlo, nessun
gentile o bestiale medicastro avendoci messo mano
per raschiarlo volontariamente (per nostra volontà) via.

Little Boy Dead from Struggling Etc.

1

The door closed behind him, in the darkness, somewhere
between five and six years old enduring
a growth of eyes, out of nowhere,
in his back and—the ceiling rolling over on the floor
and here, and here, out on the landing (the door
closed behind him from inside) what else is there to do
but look for a way out with his head, that is to say,
to wedge it between rail and rail, on the emptiness of the stairs
strenuously failing to work it free again, precisely stopping
the beating of his heart
with an infarction: just like the grownups; this is one of the
ways.

2

Now that you've told me about it I can see
how the little boy came to die:
a medium-sized blood clot on the bathroom
floor. And you, if by some chance you were
to faint, if no one else was there
then you might bleed to death. For which
behavior, you sentimentally suggest,
he really should be thanked, no amiable
or brutal quack having lifted a single finger there
to willingly (according to our will) scrape it away.

Anche così, rifletto, si produce
un santino, l'immagine buona, propiziatoria
da appendere dall'altra parte del letto in simmetria
con quelle da trattare con gli spilli . . .

3

Ha fatto troppo l'amore, dopo, sembra
che t'abbia detto; sembra
che in questo modo i bambini si fanno — questo
lo sanno tutti — ma alle volte succede di disfarli. Con
l'amore, vedi? (non a me: è da sola che cerchi d'imbrogliarti),
con l'amore, non con l'indifferenza, il fastidio,
non con la voglia di mandarlo via . . .

4

Bambino, leggendo, morto di fatica
nella Svizzera francese o forse sbaglio a ricordare, in Piemonte —
        nei pressi
(non all'ombra, assolutamente) di
un cespuglio
o addirittura di una pietra,
questo volevo dire: che la grande madre
per avergli nascosto l'animale (e lui, a rintracciarlo, in giro
ventiquattr'ore su ventiquattro, in giro come un matto, alla fine
morto di fatica o per il troppo caldo o assiderato, alla fine
impossibilitato a distinguere)
non credeva di fare nessun male.

That's how, I imagine, they go about
producing a holy card, a lovely, propitiatory image
to hang from the other side of the bed in symmetry
with all the ones already pinned up there . . .

3

She made too much love, later on, it seems
she said to you; it seems
this is the way that babies are made—this
everybody knows—but sometimes it happens they're unmade. With
love, do you see? (not to me: you're looking to get tangled up all
        by yourself),
with love, not with indifference, irritation,
not with the desire to send him away . . .

4

A little boy (reading) dead from struggling
in French Switzerland, or maybe I misremember, in Piedmont—
        in the vicinity
(not in the shadow, absolutely) of
a thicket
or even a rock,
this is what I wanted to say: that his grandmother
in having hidden the animal from him (and he, in tracking it
        down, going round
day after day after day, going round like a lunatic, in the end
dead from struggling or overheated or frozen, in the end
it had become impossible to tell)
didn't think that she was doing any harm.

La commemorazione dei defunti

Con i tuoi, lo sappiamo, un modus
vivendi l'hai trovato. Non era né facile
né difficile, quasi non c'era scelta. Ma quei tizi di cui
non ti frega niente, carbonizzati
nella carcassa di un caccia sbocconcellati dall'uomoleone falciati
dal tifo sull'altipiano, che
salvezza c'è per te in loro? che sugo
per loro nel tuo strizzar gli occhi e indugiare
a fitte sul giornale?
Siano rimessi, dico (i morti) nel nostro impasto quotidiano, piega
    il giornale,
lascia che lontano i vivi seppelliscano i vivi.

The Commemoration of the Defunct

With your own, we know, you've hit upon
a *modus vivendi*. It was neither easy
nor hard, it was hardly even a choice. But all those guys
you don't give a crap for, charred
in the skeleton of a fighter plane, nibbled by the lion-man,
    mowed down
by typhoid on the plateau, what
lifeline is there for you in them? what gravy
for them in your squinting and lingering fitfully
over the newspaper?
Let them be remixed, I say (the dead) in our daily dough, fold up
    the newspaper,
let the living bury the living far away.

da CADENZA D'INGANNO (1957–1974)

from DECEPTIVE CADENCE (1957–1974)

Parti di requiem

per mia madre

Quadratura

Se è di questo che parliamo, e se è così
che continuano a vivere — nei morsi
d'ossido alla lamiera, o come muffa
lambendo le bottiglie —
hai ragione: si sprecano dei soldi. Ma sul conto dei morti
si tramandano ancora altre notizie:
come se rimanessero vicini
ai loro corpi, incerti, diffidando
di una provvisoria corruzione,
aspettando segnali . . . E allora vedi
che i conti tornerebbero, più in là.

Creditori

Cerchiamo di parlare
in due minuti, mentre qualcuno aggiusta
le tende alle finestre e gli amici
sono gìa per le scale. Sempre c'è
poco tempo quando dobbiamo fare
i conti con i morti. E così dico
a mia madre di aver pazienza — a lei
che vicina a morire, ancora
vuol sapere com'era la mia cena . . .

Parts of a Requiem

for my mother

Squaring

If this is what we're talking about, and if
this is the way they go on living—in
the bites of oxide in sheet metal, or
like mould grazing bottles—
you're right: we're wasting money. But on the dead's account
some other information's still bequeathed:
as if they were staying close
to their bodies, hesitant, suspicious
of a provisional corruption,
waiting for signals . . . And then you see
that the accounts would be balanced, later on.

Creditors

We try to talk
for a couple of minutes, while someone adjusts
the curtains at the windows and our friends
are already coming up the stairs. There never
seems to be enough time when we should
be settling accounts with the dead. And so I tell
my mother that she should be patient—she
who, even though she's close to dying, still
makes sure to ask me how my supper was . . .

Troppo poco profondo

Anche così ti sembra
di conoscerla: gli occhi
che guardano in dentro, la fronte
rischiarata da un acido. Non c'è
da stare allegri, è tanto se riuscite
a mettervi di fronte (una
un po' più in basso) e nel vuoto, bisbigliando
con accenti di colpa, tentare
di discolparti. — A volte non affiora
che un rocchetto di polvere, ritagli
d'una specie di plastica, ossicini . . . A cosa
serve, vorrei sapere, chi ha tempo
di interrogarli?
                    se in alto, sulla sabbia,
reclamano pale, secchielli,
si mettono a scavare.

Sezione della scala

Lì
o forse altrove, ma forse proprio lì — freccina semovente,
    baluginosa nel
percorso
un gradino dopo l'altro salivo
per godermela in pace la penombra
a fiatare nell'asciutta penombra che era
lo zero millimetrico del percorso nel buio
risalito vivo in verticale verso corte all'oscuro
cinguettare osceno fonografo della tua agonia.

Not Deep Enough

Even so, it seems to you
you know her: the eyes
that look within, the forehead
lightened by an acid. There isn't
any joy in it, it's plenty if it leads
to setting you face to face (one
a bit lower) and whispering in the emptiness
with guilty intonations, trying
to exonerate yourself.—All that surfaces
sometimes is a dusty spool, some pieces cut
from some sort of plastic, ossicles . . . And what
good does it do, I'd like to know, who has
the time to examine them?
                                        if high up, on the sand,
they're claiming pails and shovels,
they're setting up to dig.

A Section of the Staircase

There
or maybe somewhere else, but maybe right there—a small self-
      propelled arrow, flickering
along the way
I went up one step after another
so as to peacefully enjoy the half-light
to breathe in the dry half-light that was
the millimetric zero of the way in the darkness
climbing once more alive vertical toward the court to the dim
twittering obscene phonograph of your agony.

Anima

« Povera anima » ti scrivo
in stampatello — anima rimasta a far da palo
ai limiti, diciamo, della competenza territoriale
in presenza della garitta slabbrata, ventosa che
il crepuscolo incenerisce . . . Bel posto
per incontrarsi, mezzo
piattaforma spaziale mezzo pattumiera
da un lato a picco (una
discesa è ricavata)
al quale sbuca la mulattiera
opera militare dei tedeschi in parte, per anni
smangiata dalle frane
finché vien giù tutto una primavera o l'altra.

Così sia. Ma per quella
cosa che dovevo
dirti (tu viva
ancora per poco)
vedi quanto mi tocca — fino
a quando
compatirti da morta?
Che tu m'abbia voluto
tenero, sporco, impotente
affogare in un bicchiere,
che io stesso continui nel tempo a volermi come
dolcemente mutilavi
la mia persona di figlio avvicina
anime prima del giusto divise,
te ferma negli spruzzi, sulla vertigine dei pescecani
alla mia paura.

Soul

"Poor soul," I write to you
in block capitals—soul remaining to stand watch
at the borders, let's say, of the territorial jurisdiction
in the presence of a windy, decrepit guardhouse
the twilight incinerates . . . A perfect spot
for meeting, half
space platform and half garbage bin
sheer on one side (a
descent dug out anew)
to where the mule track emerges, work
done partly by the German military, eaten away
for years by landslides
until the whole thing comes down one springtime or another.

So be it. But for that
thing that I had
to tell you (you still
alive for a little while)
you see how much it touches me—how
long
must I bear your being dead?
That you wanted me to be
soft, dirty, helpless
tripping over my own feet,
that I myself go on wanting to be the way
you sweetly crippled
my filial self brings close together
souls that were severed too soon,
you steady in sprays, on the dizziness of sharks
to my fright.

Come cieco, con ansia . . .

Come cieco, con ansia, contro
il temporale e la grandine, una
dopo l'altra chiudevo
sette finestre.
Importava che non sapessi quali.
Solo all'alba, tremando,
con l'orrenda minuzia di chi si sveglia o muore,
capisco che ho strisciato
dentro il solito buio,
via San Gregorio primo piano.
Al di qua dei miei figli,
di poter dare o prendere parola.

Trasloco

Presto di mattina
a un passo dal cancello, non ricordo
se in strada o nel giardino.
Non era chiuso né aperto. Poteva
essere molto tardi. Poteva esserci vento.
Bisognava rincorrerli — gridare
slittando sulla ghiaia,
darsi slancio sui pali delle dalie,
abbattersi sui platani, volare
su tre gradini di graniglia,
svelto, più svelto! prima che qualcuno
(la Gondrand, anche allora?) bestemmiando
per troppo noce,
ansando cieco per le scale,
portasse dentro — prima la testata,

Like a Blind Man, Anxiously . . .

Like a blind man, anxiously, against
the hailstones and the thunderstorm, I closed
seven windows one
after another.
It mattered that I didn't know which ones.
Only at daybreak, shivering,
with the dreadful meticulousness of somebody waking or dying,
do I see that I was creeping
inside the usual darkness,
Via San Gregorio, first floor.
On this side of my children,
of being able to yield the floor or take it.

Moving

Early in the morning
a few steps from the gate, I don't remember
whether in the street or in the garden.
It was neither closed nor open. It might have been
very late. It might have been windy there.
It was necessary to chase them—to cry out
slipping on the gravel,
grabbing the dahlia stakes to pick up speed,
falling on the plane trees, flying
up the three sandstone steps,
hurrying, hurrying faster! before somebody
(was it Gondrand, even then?), cursing because
there was too much walnut,
panting blindly because of the stairs,
could carry in—first the headboard,

poi le molle, le sponde —
il letto di mia madre.

I cugini

Le assomigliano poco. Li vedo ai funerali,
sempre più alti, più stinti, la testa
leggerissima, come bucata,
quasi soltanto nasi e bende, ormai.

Sentito dire

In casa della nonna (di tua suocera) eri
un po' un pesce fuor d'acqua. Era diverso
quasi tutto, anche il modo
di grattugiare il pane. Di nascosto ridevano
dei tuoi parenti, nobili in malora
o venditori di dolciumi. All'alba
ti calmavi, come si calma una che ha pianto fino all'alba.

Anniversario

Chi piscia sangue, chi ha
troppi globuli bianchi nelle vene
e batte i denti nella gran calura
prega: non aver fretta, non volere
che il conto sia saldato.
Accontèntati (non è un'elemosina) di queste viscere appassite, di
questi fiori.

then the springs, the sides—
my mother's bed.

The Cousins

They don't look much like her. I see them at funerals,
always taller, more faded, with their heads
very light, as though perforated,
mostly all noses and bandages, by now.

Hearsay

In grandmother's house (your mother-in-law's) you were
a bit of a fish out of water. Almost everything
was different, even the way
they grated bread. They laughed behind your back
at your relatives, nobility in tatters
or candy-store proprietors. At dawn
you calmed down, as someone calms down who has wept until
dawn.

Anniversary

Whoever pisses blood, whoever
has too many white corpuscles in the veins,
whose teeth are chattering in the blazing heat,
prays: don't be in a hurry, don't desire
the account to be settled.
Be content (it's not charity) with these withered viscera, these
flowers.

La bara

Mi chiedo se una bara
può essere così calda, davvero, come è stato
questa notte in un sogno —
dico calda da dentro se per ridere
cerco di sollevarla, se la tolgo
al furgone, alla fossa,
se l'abbraccio, sapendo nel legno che sei viva.

Amen

Quando sei morta stavamo
in una casa vecchia. L'ascensore non c'era. C'era spazio
da vendere per pianerottoli e scale.
Dunque non t'è toccato di passare
di spalla in spalla per angoli e fessure,
d'essere calcolata a spanne, raddrizzata
nel senso degli stipiti. Sparire
era più lento e facile quando tu sei sparita.
Parecchie volte, dopo, mi è sembrata
una bella fortuna.
Eppure, se ci pensi, in poche cose
c'è meno dignità che nella morte,
meno bellezza. Scendi a pianterreno
come ti pare, porta o tubo, infilati
dove capita, scatola di scarpe
o cassa d'imballaggio, orizzontale
o verticale, sola o in compagnia,
liberaci dall'estetica e così sia.

(1957–1974)

The Coffin

I ask myself if a coffin
could really be so warm, the way it was
in a dream tonight—
I say warm from the inside if for a laugh
I try to lift it, if I take it away
from the van, from the grave,
if I embrace it, knowing in the wood that you're alive.

Amen

When you died we were living
in an old house. The elevator wasn't there. There was room
to spare along the landings and the staircases.
So there was no need for you to shoulder
your way through crevices and corners,
to measure yourself in spans, drawn up straight
in awareness of the doorjambs. Disappearing
was slower and easier when you disappeared.
Many times, later on, that seemed to me
a piece of good luck.
And yet, if you think of it, there are few things
in which there is less dignity than death,
less beauty. Come down to the ground floor
just as you please, by door or duct, squeeze in
wherever it happens, shoebox
or packing case, horizontal
or vertical, alone or in company,
deliver us from aesthetics and let it be.

(1957–1974)

L'intoppo

Segni ch'i ò presi a l'amoroso intoppo
Rer. Vulg. Fragm., *LXXXVIII, 8*

Un sogno

Ho pensato che non io ma mio padre era
la persona ad amarti. Gli sorridevo nel sogno con
delicata complicità. Nel sogno era una scuola
frequentata due anni da me ragazzo,
adesso da tuo figlio.

Cosa

Mi chiedi « cosa ti piace di me, cosa
più del resto ». Una volta, per ridere
ho detto il cappellino. Però pensando
la schiena, le ginocchia: e al labbro di sopra che quasi
non tocca quello di sotto: e come
s'impenna liquido, scatta il tuo profilo.
Ma ancora di più la faccia che non sai d'avere
dopo aver fatto l'amore, netta per saliva e sudore,
a una calma che c'era rifiorita.

Raccordo

Risulti
di raccordo o scarico o d'altro il tubo
che corre basso la città
resta il fatto che non una ma due

The Impediment

Marks I received from love's impediment
Rer. Vulg. Fragm., *LXXXVIII, 8*

A Dream

I thought that not I but my father was
the person who loved you. I smiled at him in the dream with
delicate complicity. In the dream there was a school
that I went to for two years when I was a boy,
where your son goes now.

What

You ask me, "What do you like about me, more
than any other thing?" Once, for a laugh
I said your hat. Thinking it over, though,
your back, your knees: and your upper lip that almost
doesn't touch the lower one: and the way
your profile lifts like liquid splashing up.
But even more the face that you don't know
you have after making love, cleansed by sweat and saliva,
to a stillness that has flowered there once more.

Connection

Whether by
connection or unloading or by something else the tube
that runs under the city
the fact remains that not once but

volte (già sul pavimento, io, di gomma scura
tu scendendo con minuziosa calma le scale)
eravamo là sotto
nel mattino di pseudoprimavera. E che
da due giornate una
d'improvviso saltando fuori
eccoci alle presenti tenerezze, al verme
dolcissimo che ci fa fuori la vita e non fa
conto così presto di non aver fame.

Specchio

Hai le tue storie: di rivali e cognati baroni
a Palermo e letti col baldacchino
dove in uno, una volta che eri
ragazza, ti svegli bruciata.
Ho le mie storie: di bisnonni e prozii d'alto colletto
invischiati con l'Austria e decorose
darsene a lago — io così
detesto che un mobile non sia scuro e di noce.
Ma se in mezzo allo specchio con la cornice dorata, in
mezzo, nel buio dello specchio ci sei tu . . .

Sonno

L'alto sonno quando sei stanca
di stare in piedi troppo o per l'amore e collabori
alla matrigna che inviperisce nuda, all'uomo
morto che ti fa l'occhiolino (e
« cosa vorrà dire » domattina « cosa »
con ricorso alla cabala o chissà)

twice (I already on the platform of hard rubber
you coming down the stairs with meticulous calm)
we were down there
in the pseudospringtime morning. And of the two
days one suddenly
jumping out here we are
at the present tendernesses, at the sweetest
worm who takes us out of life and who
doesn't expect to not be hungry this early.

Mirror

You have your stories: of rival and brother-in-law barons
in Palermo and four-poster canopied beds
in one of which, once when you were
a girl, you wake up burned.
I have my stories: of high-collared great-grandfathers and great
uncles entangled with Austria and dignified
docks on the lake—and that's why I
hate it when furniture's not dark and made of walnut.
But if in the middle of the mirror with the gilded frame, in
the middle, in the darkness of the mirror there is you . . .

Sleep

The deep sleep when you're tired
from being on your feet too much or from love and you
    collaborate
with the stepmother who rages naked, with the dead
man who slips you a wink (and
"what does it mean" tomorrow morning "what"
with recourse to the Kabbala or who knows what)

schioccando piano-umido la bocca, mandando
quel niente di profumo
a me che non riesco a dormire, quanta
rabbia, che pena suscita di me che non riesco a dormire
se non sono a casa mia, nel mio letto!

Le volte

Dei rimproveri che mi fai (certi
non li discuto)
ce n'è uno quando arriva che fa
male come il freddo sulle dita — quando
commenti soave « che brutto amore abbiam fatto » o peggio
        « stavolta
l'amore l'hai fatto solo tu: come un ragazzino ». Morde
dal basso, asciuga saliva come se portasse
via tutte le volte buone. E dire che tengo
più alla tua gioia che alla mia; a momenti vorrei
essere una donna per toccarti meglio, con più dolcezza . . .

Posto

Si raggrinzisce
la città, perde sugo e odore la sua buccia se solo
pensassi di lasciarti. Non ci sarà
posto per camminare. Picchierò la testa contro i lampioni.
La crescita di foglie nei viali una cosa
che raspa in gola e mi fa vomitare.

softly-moistly smacking your mouth, wafting
that trifle of perfume
to me who can't get to sleep, such
fury, what pain aroused in me who can't get to sleep
if I'm not in my own house, in my own bed!

Times

Of those things you reproach me for (some of which
I don't dispute)
there's one of them that when it comes it hurts
like fingers stinging with the cold—when
you gently observe "what nasty love we just made" or worse "this
time
you were making love all by yourself: just like a kid." It bites
from below, dries my mouth as if it had taken away
all the good times. And to think that I'm more concerned
with your pleasure than my own; there are moments I'd like
to be a woman to touch you better, with more tenderness . . .

Place

The city
shrivels, its rind loses juice and fragrance if I were
just to think of leaving you. There won't be
any place to walk. I'll beat my head against the lampposts.
The blooming of leaves in the avenues a thing
that scrapes inside my throat and makes me vomit.

I manifesti

Chissà dov'ero, dove m'ero ficcato quando
le tue gambe hanno invaso la città.
Forse non guardo i manifesti.
Adesso paziente, maniaco ti do la caccia
di stazione in stazione
borbottando preghiere. Quello che non sei tu
esce dal fuoco o indietreggia se le tue
magre, livide dita si vede che una calza
tendono con increscioso pudore.

Le iniziali

Nati
sotto lo stesso segno
credo l'acquario, è un fatto che a rigore
d'anagrafe e precisa
distanza avendo
le stesse due iniziali
ma rovesciate, così — tu da sempre (da sempre!) a oscuri
scolastici schemi, sollecitazioni t'ostini a dar retta
e metti il cognome davanti al nome.

Supina

Se ti metti supina
diventa, calmandosi, solo dolcezza
il peso del tuo seno. Di colpo non c'è
bisogno di nasconderlo, non si può più giocare perché è tenero e
spento
e innocente e basta.

The Posters

Who knows where I was, where I had stuck myself
when those two legs of yours invaded the city.
Maybe I don't keep an eye on the posters.
Now patient, maniacal I chase after you
from station to station
muttering prayers. What isn't you
goes out of focus or falls back if your thin
and livid fingers are seen to be pulling up
a stocking with regrettable modesty.

The Initials

Born
under the same sign
Aquarius I believe, it's a fact that by the strictness
of the registry office and exact
distance having
the same two initials
but reversed, like so—you, since always (since always!) persist
in heeding obscure scholastic schemes and solicitations,
and go on putting your last name before your first.

Supine

If you lie supine
the weight of your breasts becomes, as they
grow calm, pure sweetness. All at once there is
no need to hide it, one can't play anymore because it's tender and
    spent
and innocent and that's enough.

Del gridare

La cosa che a te si rompe dentro di colpo precisa nella
parte alta del gridare, del ridere soprattutto
(spiega l'altro tranquillo: difetto delle corde vocali)
dovrebbe farti capire, no? dovrebbe
metterti sulla strada per capire
l'urto che m'abbassa netto il cuore, mi stràngola se
penso quello che avendo si può perdere.

Generalmente

Eppure
non ci credo, d'accordo ma non riesco a crederci a pensarci che lui
ieri o domani o in un punto qualsiasi del tempo dello spazio
        generalmente qualcuno
abbia cose da dire progetti ipotesi da formulare su
cose che io solo furbo che sono
posso capire in
parte avendole inventate al limite — su come
sono precise sottili alle giunture le tue braccia e il muso

e muso e ginocchia da bambina, anima mia.

(1965)

Of the Scream

The thing that suddenly breaks inside you precisely in
the top of a scream, of a laugh especially
(the tranquil other explains: a defect of the vocal cords)
ought to make you understand, not so? it ought
to put you on the road to understanding
the shock that makes my heart drop sharply, that chokes me if
I think that having means that one can lose.

In General

And yet
I don't believe it, granted but I can't believe it think it that he
yesterday or tomorrow or at any point of time of space in general
        someone
has things to say projects hypotheses to formulate about
things that I alone sly as I am
can understand in
part by having imagined them to the limits—about how
precise slender at the joints are your arms and the face

and face and knees of a little girl, my heart.

(1965)

La morìa

1

L'acqua
stata alta da poco — « ma no, non questo, forse »
(sgombravano la piazza, tiravano su le assi)
« forse l'idea d'esserci andati
per una cosa, per fare quella cosa e basta »
nel tempo che cerco d'organizzarmi tu vai avanti
imperterrita « o più semplicemente
che non mi piacesse l'albergo? » Ti liberi. Fai venire
voglia, ancora una volta, di metterti il sale sulla coda.

2

« Non perderemo il treno? » La valigia
è quasi pronta, mancano ore. « Dai, mettiamo
a posto il letto, non devono capire
che anche oggi, mi secca. » Con il palmo
della mano si normalizza il lenzuolo si rettifica si
sciolgono umide impronte. « Stamattina
ai telefoni, ti giuro, non posso, non posso, io
non posso raccontare delle balle a mia figlia. »

The Plague

1

The water
risen not long before—"but no, not this, maybe"
(they were emptying out the square, pulling up the boards)
"maybe the idea of having gone there
for one thing, to do that thing and that's it,"
while I try to pull myself together you press on
undeterred, "or more simply that
I might not like the hotel?" You free yourself. You make me
feel, one more time, like putting salt on your tail.

2

"Won't we miss the train?" The suitcase
is almost packed, we still have hours. "Look, we should
make up the bed, they don't need to see
that even today, it bothers me." With the palm
of the hand the sheets are smoothed and straightened, the
damp impressions are brushed away. "This morning
at the telephones, I swear to you, I can't, I can't, I
just can't tell my daughter a pack of lies."

3

Non inatteso. Sfigurato. « Me l'immagino
la tua passeggiata, il fango
sotto i ponti, l'odore di morìa.
Conosco le facciate che hai visto. Rasento
il numero delle coltellate. Ma non era
che fosse rimorso, ma che eri sola . . . »
« Credi quello che vuoi,
pensami incerta o debole o una
che legge troppe storie e si confonde
più del normale. Io credo che è da qui
che comincia, dove comincia a finire. »

4

Non sogno. Non mi capita più di sognare.
I pacifici oggetti mimetizzati sotto frasche o teli,
i bagliori d'acciaio senza acume
sono dunque avviati su binari morti.
Eppure: meno male, pensavo, siamo arrivati sotto la tettoia
prima che i provocatori siano morti,
in modo irrimediabile lenito l'acciaio,
acciaccate le punte che ci vogliono morti. Il freddo
è appena freddo, i rombi
di luce sull'asfalto traslano piano,
la città non si vede. « Ecco, è così che sono, adesso
l'hai visto » — proprio le volte che non mi sembri vera.

(1967)

3

Not unexpected. Disfigured. "I picture
your walk in my mind, the mud
under the bridges, the odor of the plague.
I know the façades you've seen. I brush over
the number of the stab wounds. But it wasn't
that there was remorse, but that you were alone."
"Think what you like,
call me delicate or unsteady or say I'm a woman
who reads too many stories and gets abnormally
confused. I think that from here on it begins,
that here is the beginning of the end."

4

I'm not dreaming. I don't happen to dream anymore.
The peaceful objects camouflaged under branches or canvas,
the flashes of steel without sharpness
are therefore being shunted onto the sidings.
And yet: thank goodness, I thought, we made it under the
    platform
shelter before the troublemakers had died,
the steel been irremediably dulled,
the points weakened that wanted us dead. The cold
is barely cold, the rhombs
of light are moving slowly over the asphalt,
you can't see the city. "Look, this is how I am, now
you've seen it"—precisely the times you don't seem real to me.

(1967)

Soppressione

« Un medico di Auschwitz » ci era parso
la prima volta. Alla fine (visite trattative
e il resto) un buon diavolo zoppo. Guardarsi col sorriso
di chi vorrebbe non esserci o vomitare
era affar nostro dopotutto e neutro
il terreno, gabbia dell'ascensore
o pianerottolo. Al di là della porta era affar suo. Al di là della
        porta
è affar suo tutto quanto, a cominciare
dagli scrupoli bruschi che non riuscivo a provare. « In coscienza
li sconsiglio — no, non è più difficile, è una cosa
diversa: al primo mese è un conto: c'è una specie
di bambino, adesso, da fare a pezzi. » Guardava la vetrina
con i ferri parlando oppure chi
sarà stato a guardarla? Sì, peccato volevo
dirgli, peccato, non ci pensi, si faccia coraggio.

Vetrina d'alghe. Vetrina
d'alberi nani. Nel sonno, ricapitolato, quel poco
verde della città.
Superficialmente nel sonno si divide la nostra storia.
Al Parco, dicevo, ci sono i mostri; ai Giardini i soldati.

Non così neutro in fondo — una gabbia che sale
lentissima dentro blocchi di luce. Niente è stato difficile, c'è
        stato
posto per la macchina davanti al portone,

Suppression

“An Auschwitz doctor” so he seemed to us
the first time. In the end (visits negotiations
and the rest) not a bad fellow, with a limp. Exchanging the smiles
of people who wish they were somewhere else or vomiting
was our concern after all and the ground
neutral, an elevator cage
or landing. On the other side of the door it was his concern. On
    the other
side of the door it’s all his concern, starting with
the rough scruples that I couldn’t feel. “In good conscience
I advise against it—no, it’s not more difficult, it’s something
else: in the first month it’s a consideration: there’s a sort
of a baby, now, to cut to pieces.” He was looking at the glass case
with the instruments while he talked, otherwise who
would there have been to look at it? Yes, it’s a pity I wanted
to tell him, a pity, don’t think about it, be brave.

Glass case of algae. Glass case
of dwarf trees. In sleep, recapitulated, that little
bit of green in the city.
Superficially in sleep our story is divided.
In the Park, I said, there are the monsters; in the Gardens the
    soldiers.

Not so neutral after all—a cage that rises
slowly, slowly through blocks of light. Nothing’s been hard,
    there’s been
a parking space right in front of the entrance,

ordine d'immondizie nel cortile. Al silenzio
che ci accorcia lo stomaco (e: cretino, pensavo,
cretino, bestia, come hai fatto a cascarci un'altra volta?)
ci sarà pure da qualche parte qualcosa
da dare in pasto, torpido animale
a quattro zampe, confusa persona plurale . . .

(1968)

trash neatly piled in the courtyard. In the silence
that tightens our stomachs (and: idiot, I was thinking,
idiot, beast, how have you managed to land here once again?)
there will still be something somewhere
for fodder, a dull animal
on all fours, a confused person plural . . .

(1968)

Inchiesta

ore 14.30

« Tutto quello che so? Non ero
ancora nata allora. » Ma da quando — il marito
morto nel '37, i figli vivi
a Aquisgrana, a Zurigo — da quanto tempo a sciogliere e legare
nastri e spaghi, a accarezzare sigilli?
« Sì, figùrati, rogiti di case
disfatte da cent'anni, odi per nozze
di cantanti o granduchi, pergamene
con nomi da pastore;
e di dopo anche meno, qualche foto,
qualche lettera insulsa. » Ma in mezzo, dentro, come
la puntura dell'insetto invischiato, l'amo nel semolino,
come . . . « Lo sai che non si scrivono
queste cose: non certo fra parenti. »

ore 19

Somiglianze discusse a colpi di candela
nelle stanze alte, piene di stipiti;
pazzesco: non un vetro che chiuda: e l'autunno
che sembra inverno, macera i campanili . . .
Già fra cugini, e con dispensa, il sangue
s'assottiglia, rischia d'andare in acqua; ma così!
« Così come? » Serve e gatti avvelenano la cena
dello scapolo leggero d'ossa,

Inquiry

2:30 p.m.

"Everything I know? I wasn't
even born then." But from when—the husband
dead in '37, the children living
in Aix-la-Chapelle, in Zurich—from how far back to loosen and tie
ribbons and twine, to stroke the wax seals?
"Yes, just imagine, deeds to houses
torn down a hundred years ago, odes for the marriages
of singers or grand dukes, parchments
with pastors' names;
and from later on even less, a few photographs,
a few insipid letters." But in the middle, inside, like
the sting of the trapped insect, the fishhook in the semolina,
like . . . "You know that people don't write
such things: and certainly not among relatives."

7:00 p.m.

Likenesses debated by flickering candlelight
in the upstairs rooms, with doorjambs everywhere;
unreal: not a single window that closes: and a fall
that feels like winter, that macerates the bell towers . . .
Between cousins, and with dispensation, the blood
already thins out, in danger of turning to water; but like this!
"Like what?" Servants and cats poison the dinner
of the delicate-boned bachelor

disposto a consunzione. Più giù la biacca s'altera, sprofonda
il prefetto codino, la nipote
del cardinale. Non è molto quello che so.

ore 23

Color seppia. 9 x 16. Spessore 2 mm. Penso
ingrandimenti progressivi, reticoli, lo sfondo
che si schiarisce, si sgrana, ho
una lente quadrata per francobolli, una
lampadina mignon da 25 candele, l'ombra
cade dalla parte sbagliata, l'occhio che mi balla sempre un po' a
    quest'ora.

ore 23.15

La mano grande, pacata,
la grande mano pacata si posa
dietro i balbuzienti, miti,
le occhiate bianche, le bocche sottili disposte a,
nella parte alta del gruppo, dietro
i piccoli crani, le tempie visibilmente pulsanti e leggere,
le orecchie che vibrano incerte in attesa
della buffa dissoluzione finale, del comico inchino,
nel rettangolo alto destro nel punto
d'intersezione verticale del vertice
della piramide delle minori
biancastre miti consultazioni di sguardi,
ossario infantile, docili, visibilmente disposti a consunzione,
dietro la labile precoce lapide di
bambini che aspettano la dissoluzione

prone to consumption. Lower down white lead alters, overcomes
the old fogey prefect, the cardinal's
niece. What I know isn't very much.

11:00 p.m.

Sepia-colored. 4x5. A twelfth of an inch thick. I think
progressive enlargements, grids, the background
getting lighter, grainy, I have
a square lens for postage stamps, a tiny
25-candlepower lamp, the shadow
falls on the wrong side, my eye that's always a little jittery at this
hour.

11:15 p.m.

The large hand, calm,
the large calm hand rests behind
the stammerers, the mild ones,
the blank expressions, the thin mouths prone to,
in the upper part of the group, behind
the little skulls, the light and visibly throbbing temples,
the ears quivering uncertainly waiting for
the final droll dissolution, the comic curtsey and bow,
in the upper right rectangle at the point
of the vertical intersection of the vertex
of the pyramid of the minor
whitish mild consultations of glances,
infant ossuary, meek, visibly prone to consumption,
behind the fleeting premature tombstone of
the children waiting for the dissolution

del gruppo, la risata servile
del fotografo, il ripiegamento del trespolo conseguenti
allo scoppio al fumo la mano
adulta, la grande mano piccola d'ossa si posa
sul guanto sottile sulle dita docili minute d'ossa tremanti chiuse
sull'avorio (possibile; color seppia) dell'ombrellino.

(1968)

of the group, the obsequious laughter
of the photographer, the folding up of the tripod following
the explosion and the smoke, the adult
hand, the large small-boned hand rests
on the thin glove on the meek minutely-boned trembling fingers
    closed
on the ivory (possible; sepia-colored) of the parasol.

(1968)

Il compleanno di mia figlia

Siano con selvaggia compunzione accese
le tre candele.
Saltino sui coperchi con fragore i dui
compari di spada compiuti uno
sei anni e mezzo, l'altro cinque
e io trentaquattro e la mamma trentadue
e la nonna, se non sbaglio, sessantotto.
Questa scena non verrà ripetuta.
La scena non viene diversamente effigiata. E chi
si sentisse esule o in qualche
percentuale risulta ingrugnato
parli prima o domani.
Accogli, streghina di marzapane, la nostra sospettosa tenerezza.
Seguano come a caso stridi
di vagoni piombati, raffiche di mitragliatrice . . .

(1966)

My Daughter's Birthday

Let the three candles be lighted with primitive
compunction.
Let the two brothers in arms jump on the covers
and make a racket, one of them being
six and a half, the other one five
and I thirty-four and mama thirty-two
and grandma sixty-eight, if I'm not mistaken.
This is a scene that won't be reenacted.
The scene's not depicted otherwise. And if
anyone felt exiled or starts
to pout in any percentage
let him speak earlier or tomorrow.
Accept, little marzipan witch, our suspicious affection.
Let follow as if at random screeches
of plunging trains, bursts of machine-gun fire . . .

(1966)

L'alibi del morto

Giuda dice che l'alibi del morto
era crollato: per questo il morto è sceso nel cortile.
Ma l'alibi era buono; il morto è riabilitato:
nessuno dice che Giuda aveva torto.

Il perito settore dice che le ferite
non sono imcompatibili con la meccanica di
una caduta dall'alto. Il giornale conclude
che dunque il morto si è suicidato.

Miserabili vecchi che per pietà
di se stessi dovrebbero esser morti
ci parlano dagli specchi, ci ammoniscono, ci insegnano il futuro,
escono dagli specchi per baciare i morti.

L'assassino s'è affrettato a sparlare del morto.
S'era sentito un assassino compatire un morto.
S'era visto un assassino baciare la fronte di un morto.
Vedi che gli assassini non trascurano i morti.

20.30 cordoglio del beone
20.31 rampogne del furfante
20.32 consigli dell'idiota
20.33 ultimatum del boia.

The Dead Man's Alibi

Judas says that his alibi was shaken,
the dead man's: that's why the dead man went down to the
courtyard.
But the alibi was sound; the dead man was rehabilitated:
nobody says that Judas was mistaken.

The medical examiner says that the wounds
are not incompatible with the mechanics of
a fall from a high place. The newspaper concludes
that therefore the dead man was a suicide.

Miserable old men who out of pity
for themselves ought to be dead
talk to us out of mirrors, warn us, show us the future,
come out of mirrors in order to kiss the dead.

The killer was quick to speak ill of the dead man.
A killer was heard to sympathize with a dead man.
A killer was seen to kiss the forehead of a dead man.
You see that killers don't disregard the dead.

8:30 p.m. the drunkard's lamentation
8:31 the scoundrel's castigation
8:32 the imbecile's advice
8:33 the hangman's ultimatum

La Borsa è sana, la Borsa reagisce
con splendido, inatteso, confortante vigore
alle notizie dal fronte, ai proclami, alla limpida morte
del legionario ucciso dal nemico.

Corvi senz'ali all'ombra
piatta della bilancia
trinità di sicari
brandiscono la lancia.

Giuda dice: la gente ai miei guerrieri
ha buttato dei sassi, per questo han caricato.
Di chi c'era nessuno se n'è accorto:
ma il Senato decide che Giuda non ha torto.

Non predicate la dittatura
di una classe sull'altra, non è il vostro lavoro.
Non dite niente che possa suscitare
l'odio di classe: ci pensano già loro.

Parlo per me ma forse anche per voi.
Amici, diciamo la verità:
di sentirci oppressi ci sentiamo felici;
ci importa adesso esser vittime, non esser liberi poi.

(1970)

The stock market's sound, the stock market reacts
with splendid, unexpected, encouraging vigor
to the news from the front, the proclamations, the limpid death
of the legionnaire killed by the enemy.

Wingless crows in the flat
shadow of the scales
trinity of cutthroats
brandishing the spears.

Judas says: the people were casting stones
at my warriors, that's why my soldiers charged.
Of who was there it seems no notice was taken:
but the Senate decides that Judas was not mistaken.

Don't preach the dictatorship
of one class over the other, that's not your occupation.
Don't say anything that might provoke
class hatred: they've already got the notion.

I speak for myself but maybe for you as well.
Friends, let's tell the truth, I say:
It makes us happy when we feel oppressed;
what matters is being victims now, not being free someday.

(1970)

Il gioco del mondo

1

Disegnato col gesso come era
sul marciapiede il mondo si cancella.
Mi vedo perdere colpi, avere pietà
del questore giustiziato, del carabiniere in salita.

2

Con la leggerezza di uno che sogna d'esser vivo
dopo lo scatto degli otturatori
strappo cellophane, buio
dall'arabia frizzante del mattino.

3

Mi sveglio per te, non per la luce.
Nella foresta meccanica saltano vive
le lepri, vortica carnoso
l'enorme sussiego del pavone.

(1972)

The Game of the World

1

Drawn with chalk as it was
on the sidewalk the world fades away.
I see that I'm slowing down, feeling pity for
the executed commissioner, the cop up on the hill.

2

With the lightness of someone who dreams of being alive
after the click of the shutters
I peel away cellophane, dark
from the brisk Arabia of the morning.

3

I wake up because of you, not the light.
In the mechanical forest live hares
are leaping, the enormous
haughtiness of the peacock swirls fleshily.

(1972)

Per C., morta di parto all'età di un anno e undici mesi

1

È (diceva il mio amore) mia sorella
morta dieci anni fa. La riconosco
dagli occhi di mirtillo . . .
Io le credevo. E adesso ci chiediamo
dove ti incontreremo un'altra volta,
in quale pesciolino, albero, odore.

2

Come in un libro o all'opera
sembra un trucco squisito la tua morte
preparata nei gesti della vita
con mille dolcissimi addii.

3

Nella cesta, con te, sotto il lenzuolo
a righe azzurre e bianche, un rametto di fiori
di quelli che ci piacciono,
che tu mangiavi.

For C., Dead in Childbirth at the Age of One Year and Eleven Months

1

She is (my loved one used to say) my sister
who died ten years ago. I recognize her
by her blueberry eyes . . .
I believed her. And now we ask ourselves
where we will come across you once again,
in what little fish, or tree, or scent.

2

As in a book or in an opera
your death seems an exquisite sleight of hand
that life's gestures had been leading to
with a thousand of the sweetest of farewells.

3

Inside the basket, with you, under the blue-
and-white-striped sheet, a little branch of flowers,
the ones we like, the ones
you used to eat.

4

Solo con Elsa, stamattina,
si può parlare . . . E come per miracolo
Elsa risponde, non è più partita,
ci sta a sentire, parla del dolore
di tuoi remoti fratellini,
ride persino, ci consola . . .

5

Adesso, corpicino stremato, ti riposi
in nessun posto. E noi se ci pensiamo
non sentiamo amarezza
ma la svenante, tiepida cacciata
dal paradiso.

(1974)

4

Only with Elsa, this morning,
are we able to talk . . . And as if by a miracle,
Elsa answers, she isn't away anymore,
she listens to us, she talks about the sorrow
of your far-off little brothers,
she even laughs, she consoles us . . .

5

Exhausted little body, now you rest
in no place. And if we think about it
we don't feel any bitterness
but only the bloodletting, tepid expulsion
from paradise.

(1974)

da NEL GRAVE SOGNO (1965–1981)

from IN THE HEAVY DREAM (1965–1981)

Celeste

Uno, chissà perché, con la coperta
sulle ginocchia:
a un sole d'inverno, di scarsa primavera . . .
(C'è voluto del tempo a sprofondare
dove credevo che tu fossi, gli oblò
neri di sabbia o ghiaccio.
Una volta arrivato non avevo
niente da dirti, o quasi. È stato un bene
non trovarti — se pure
c'eri mai stato.
Libero, m'affeziono allo scenario
di prima, chaises longues scrostate, portafiori
di terracotta rovesciati, e dove
dietro le rose stente s'indovina
la curva della terra,
il celeste di Lucca o Pontedera . . .)

Sky-Blue

Somebody, who knows why, sits with a blanket
over his knees,
sits in a sun of winter, of meager springtime . . .
(It took a bit of time for me to drop
below where I believed you were, the portholes
black with sand or ice.
Once I arrived I had nothing to say
to you, or nearly. It was a good thing
not to find you—if indeed
you'd ever been there.
Free, I'm growing fond of the previous
decor, the stripped chaise longues, the overturned
terracotta flowerpots, and where
behind the stunted roses you can divine
the curve of the earth,
the sky-blue of Lucca or of Pontedera . . .)

L’appartamento

1

Passa, dicono, le giornate
con addosso un pigiama, una vestaglia. A chi
gli consiglia d’uscire, di muoversi, altrimenti
i muscoli, alla sua età, si atrofizzano, le giunture
si bloccano, risponde
con un dolce, lento sorriso.

2

Caverna, bunker, mucosa,
spolverati libri che nessuno
leggerà né scompiglia,
grande schermo millimetrato della concentrazione,
dell’introiezione — e dovrebbe
spegnerlo, vestirsi, arrischiare le ossa
nell’aria confusa, piena di pòlline?

3

Va piano piano alla finestra
a vedere se nevica ancora, se continua
nel buio luminoso, là fuori
l’infantile disastro del mondo.

The Apartment

1

He spends his days, they say,
wearing a pair of pajamas, a bathrobe. To everyone
who tells him to go outside, to bestir himself, otherwise
his muscles, at his age, will atrophy, his joints
will seize up, he responds
with a sweet, slow smile.

2

Cave, bunker, mucous membrane,
dusted books that no one
will read or disarrange,
large screen calibrated in millimeters of concentration,
of introjection—and should he
turn it off, dress himself, and risk his bones
out in the messy, pollen-laden air?

3

He goes ever so slowly to the window
to see if it's still snowing, if it's still going on
in the luminous darkness out there,
the infantile disaster of the world.

Personcina

Quando dorme se lo chiami
muove un orecchio solo.

Succhia latte nei sogni
dalla sua mamma morta.

Morde biscotti. Adora
i fondi di caffè.

Con le zampe assapora
scialli e maglioni.

Dorme sui fogli. Usa
un libro per cuscino.

Sta bene soprattutto
in fondo agli armadi, nelle scatole . . .

Con occhi più verdi, tremando
spia il viavai dei piccioni.

Si lecca i baffi puntando
la mosca che volerà.

Little Person

Call him while he's sleeping
and he only flicks an ear.

He suckles in his dreams
at his dead mama's breast.

He gnaws biscuits. He adores
the taste of coffee grounds.

With his paws he savors
shawls and thick pullovers.

He sleeps on stacks of paper.
He uses books as cushions.

He's in his element
in the bottoms of cupboards, in boxes . . .

Eyes greener, he quivers, marking
the to and fro of pigeons.

He licks his whiskers stalking
the fly that'll fly away.

Interni clinica

a Bartolo Cattafi

1

. . . Il batticuore
di sempre quando aspetto
di partire da solo — non sarà,
mi dico, così diversa la morte,
questa tua per esempio, alla moviola,
corteggiata, covata come un uovo,
sera dopo sera discussa con gli amici
come una battaglia da perdere tardi, con onore . . .

2

Vampa, vetrofanie del crepuscolo
e dentro, accartocciato,
radioso, l'uomo malato, il ragazzo malato che cerca di dribblare
lo stopper della morte
con il numero fantastico dei minuti in un giorno,
dei giorni in una vita . . .

3

« Non lasciatemi solo . . . » E: « Sapeste
quanto bene mi ha fatto! »
E ancora, da dietro la porta
socchiusa, mentre andiamo

Interiors: Clinic

to Bartolo Cattafi

1

. . . The palpitations
as always when I'm waiting
to go away alone—death,
I tell myself, won't be so different,
this one of yours, for instance, in slow motion,
courted, brooded over like an egg,
talked over with friends evening after evening
as a battle to be lost late, with honor . . .

2

A blaze, the window decals in the twilight
and inside, shriveled,
radiant, the sick man, the sick boy who's looking to dribble
past death's goaltender
with the fantastic number of minutes in a day,
of days in a life . . .

3

"Don't leave me all alone . . ." And: "If you knew
how much good it's done me!"
And again, from behind the half-
closed door, while we make our way

contriti nel bianco verso l'ascensore:
« Grazie. Vi aspetto! »
Ah povero amico, cosa ci sarà
più da aspettare? Vedo
che cerchi gli occhiali, a tastoni, adagio, attento
a non perdere il filo dell'ossigeno,
a scansare bottiglie, medicine — e
ecco, occhiali sul naso perlustrare
la penombra, adorare
il decrepito corpo della luce,
gli ultimi, frusti bagliori degli spigoli . . .
Niente, più niente da aspettare . . .
Eppure lo so (adesso
che sei morto lo so)
è ancora una persona la tua, un astuto
labirinto dove la vita
entra e esce, un monumento
di specchietti girevoli, una macchina
delicata, stupenda . . . Quanta vita
nel tuo farcela appena,
nella ghiaia, nelle spine del tuo fiato . . .

contritely through the whiteness toward the elevator:
"Thanks. I'll be expecting you!"
Ah, poor friend, what will there be
to expect anymore? I see
you looking for your glasses, groping, gentle, careful
not to lose the line of oxygen,
to steer clear of the bottles, the medicine—and
look, your glasses on your nose to reconnoiter
the shadow, to adore
the decrepit body of the light,
the last worn glimmers of the corners . . .
Nothing, nothing more to expect . . .
And yet I know (now
that you are dead I know it)
that yours is still a self, a sly
labyrinth where life
goes in and out, a monument
of small revolving mirrors, a delicate
magnificent machine . . . So much life
in your barely hanging on,
in the gravel, in the sharp thorns of your breath . . .

Le custodi

Sceso tremando, con dolore.
Ma dove, a pensarci, m'aspettavo
i singulti dei bozzoli, l'ansia dell'albume
fiotta copiosa la letizia
delle custodi del caldo, materne umide cagne
dalle orecchie puntute, dallo sguardo
lento, terroso. Non bisogna,
anime care, lamentarsi
di voi, del fango che insieme, a poco a poco,
cavate dal profondo. Né ridendo
rinnegarvi nel mondo
che su al fresco semplifica, sragiona . . .

The Guardians

Descended trembling, with pain.
But where, in thinking of it, I expected
the sobs of cocoons, the anxiety of albumen
joy flows out copiously, the joy
of the guardians of the warm, the damp maternal dogs
with pointed ears, with earthy lingering
glances. There's no need,
dear spirits, to complain
of you, of the mud that together, bit by bit,
you dig up from the deep. Or, laughing, to
renounce you in the world
that simplifies and babbles up in the cool open air . . .

Frasi

Non so se chiamarlo
vuoto d'aria o dolore
questo cadere
dall'ovale dei bisbigli
nel quadrato del suono

Quando aderiva
ai tendini, alle ossa, e
era calma, splendente . . .

Poltrone a strappi, d'incerata . . .
Nei corridoi, braccato dagli spifferi,
l'ubriaco sbaglia porta,
il morto cammina come un ubriaco

Nel corridoio dove
c'è troppa luce arranca, si puntella,
trascina le ciabatte — un vecchio! un vecchio! — assorto
nei bisbigli, braccato dagli spifferi . . .

Rintrona, covo algido, squama . . .

Povero micio, ritornello
flebile — e intanto
liscia il crapino tenero, ammaccato, d'uccello, di serpente, su
bisbigli brancolando

Phrases

I wonder should I call it
air pocket or pain
this fall
from the oval of whispers
into the square of sound

When it clung
to the tendons, the bones, and
was calm, glittering . . .

Tattered armchairs, oilcloth-covered . . .
In the hallways, hounded by drafts,
the drunk takes the wrong door,
the dead man walks like a drunk

In the hallway where
there's too much light, he hobbles, props himself,
drags his ratty slippers—an old man! an old man!—absorbed
in whispers, hounded by drafts . . .

It thunders, algid lair, metal flake . . .

Poor kitty, a feeble
refrain—and meanwhile
he strokes the tender, dented little noggin of a bird, a snake,
        groping
over the whispers

Un giallo un viola di brughiera
ardono ciechi
nel latte del crepuscolo

A yellow a violet on the heather
are burning blind
in the milk of twilight

Le nozze

Non ho grandi pretese. M'accontento
d'essere l'uomo vestito d'azzurro, o di rosso, che si specchia
fra schiena e schiena, sfuocato, dolcemente
fungibile — l'azzurro
o il rosso, non importa
quale —
nella ruota lobata della passione.
Johannes fuit hic. Non
nel suo sguardo d'albino,
nella mano di cera che tocca la tua mano.

Dunque non ha finestre la camera nuziale.
O
la listarella bianca, sghemba, l'oro
delle mele rachitiche che sale,
freddo, dal campiello invisibile . . .
Con fini
ceree falangi predica, prepara
la consunzione dei velluti, la posizione
futura degli scheletri.

In nessun luogo, mai, tanti Giovanni — sotto
copricapi di panno, di castoro
e drappi, e spavaldi turbanti — per un solo
spasmo d'alba o di luna
di cui, preghi, non una

The Wedding

I have no grand pretensions. I content myself
with being the man dressed in blue, or red, who is reflected
between back and back, unfocused, softly
fungible—the blue one
or the red, it doesn't matter
which—
in the lobed wheel of the Passion.
Johannes fuit hic. Not
in his albino look,
in the wax hand that is touching your hand.

Then there are no windows in the bridal chamber.
                                                                                Or
the narrow, crooked white strip, the gold
of rachitic apples that rises,
cold, from the invisible *campiello* . . .
                                                            With thin
waxy phalanges he preaches, arranges
the consumption of the velvets, the future
position of the skeletons.

Never in one place so many Giovannis—under
headgear of cloth, of beaver fur
and silks, and haughty turbans—for a single
spasm of moonlight or dawn
of which, you pray, not one

goccia si versi
sul lucido impiantito
né scenda, nastrino di sangue,
a cingerti la gola
finché vita non vi separi.

Adesso, sola, nella sproporzione dei capelli
sul liscio e gracile torso nudo, sulla funebre gola,
t'asciughi il ventre, oscilli
come un calice o un flauto tra l'ancella e il catino,
ferma, eretta, teneramente
donna più giù della vita
e neanche, credo, t'accorgi dei serpenti
che leccano l'ovale dei capezzoli,
tutta fuori di mente nell'attesa
di ciò che è stato.

drop will spill
on the polished floor
or descend, a ribbon of blood,
to encircle your throat
till life do you part.

Alone, now, in the disproportion of your hair
on your smooth and slim bare torso, on your funereal throat,
you wipe your belly, you sway
like a chalice or a flute between the handmaid and the basin,
firm, upright, tenderly
woman further below the waist
and neither, I think, do you perceive the serpents
that lick the oval of your nipples,
all of it far from your mind while waiting
for what has been.

CANZONETTE MORTALI (1981–1983)

MORTAL CANZONETTES (1981–1983)

Canzonette mortali

Io che ho sempre adorato le spoglie del futuro
e solo del futuro, di nient'altro
ho qualche volta nostalgia
ricordo adesso con spavento
quando alle mie carezze smetterai di bagnarti,
quando dal mio piacere
sarai divisa e forse per bellezza
d'essere tanto amata o per dolcezza
d'avermi amato
farai finta lo stesso di godere.

Le volte che è con furia
che nel tuo ventre cerco la mia gioia
è perché, amore, so che più di tanto
non avrà tempo il tempo
di scorrere equamente per noi due
e che solo in un sogno o dalla corsa
del tempo buttandomi giù prima
posso fare che un giorno tu non voglia
da un altro amore credere l'amore.

Un giorno o l'altro ti lascio, un giorno
dopo l'altro ti lascio, anima mia.
Per gelosia di vecchio, per paura
di perderti — o perché
avrò smesso di vivere, soltanto.

Mortal Canzonettes

I who have always cherished the future's spoils
and only the future's, for nothing else
am I nostalgic at times
now that I call to mind with fear
when you'll be no longer wet from my caress,
when you'll be removed
from my pleasure, and perhaps for the loveliness
of being so loved or the sweetness of having loved me
you might still
pretend that you enjoy it nonetheless.

Those times when with a fury
I go probing in your womb to find my joy,
my love, it is because I know that time
will not have enough time
to run at the same pace for both of us
and that only in a dream or throwing myself
out of time's race first can I be sure
that there will never be a day when you
want to believe in the love of another love.

One day or another I'm leaving you, one day
after another I'm leaving you, my soul.
Out of an old man's jealousy, out of fear
of losing you—or it will
be merely that I'll have stopped living.

Però sto fermo, intanto,
come sta fermo un ramo
su cui sta fermo un passero, m'incanto . . .

Non questa volta, non ancora.
Quando ci scivoliamo dalle braccia
è solo per cercare un altro abbraccio,
quello del sonno, della calma — e c'è
come fosse per sempre
da pensare al riposo della spalla,
da aver riguardo per i tuoi capelli.

Meglio che tu non sappia
con che preghiere m'addormento, quali
parole borbottando
nel quarto muto della gola
per non farmi squartare un'altra volta
dall'avido sonno indovino.

Il cuore che non dorme
dice al cuore che dorme: Abbi paura.
Ma io non sono il mio cuore, non ascolto
né do la sorte, so bene che mancarti,
non perderti, era l'ultima sventura.

Ti muovi nel sonno. Non girarti,
non vedermi vicino e senza luce!
Occhio per occhio, parola per parola,
sto ripassando la parte della vita.

And yet, enchanted, I am still for now,
just as a bough is still,
just as a sparrow is still upon the bough . . .

Not this time, not yet.
When we slip out of one another's arms
it's only to go in search of another embrace,
the embrace of sleep, of peacefulness—and there is
as though it were for always
the seeing to the shoulder's repose,
the consideration for your hair.

Better that you don't know
the prayers I use to put myself to sleep,
the words I'm muttering
in the silent quarter of my throat
to keep me from being quartered once again
by greedy prophetic sleep.

The heart that's not asleep
says to the heart that's sleeping: Be afraid.
But I am not my heart, I don't listen to
fate or pronounce it, I know the ultimate
misfortune was missing you, not losing you.

You stir in your sleep. Don't turn around,
don't see me near you and without the light.
Eye for eye, word for word,
I have been going over the part of life.

Penso se avrò il coraggio
di tacere, sorridere, guardarti
che mi guardi morire.

Solo questo domando: esserti sempre,
per quanto tu mi sei cara, leggero.

Ti giri nel sonno, in un sogno, a poca luce.

I wonder if I will have
the courage to keep still, to smile, to watch you
as you watch me dying.

This is all I ask: to always be for you,
as far as you are dear to me, lighthearted.

You turn in your sleep, in a dream, in the faint light.

Lista di Spagna

Ma in Ispagna . . .
Don Giovanni, *atto I*, *scena V*

L'amore
lasciato lì con le zampe
che si muovono ancora, che vorrebbero
correre, arrampicarsi chissà dove . . .

***

Pensando al tuo faccino
tondo e aguzzo guardavo le bandiere
del Tiziano dei Frari.

***

L'iperbole che ami,
quella che sei: t'adoro
nella curva dei fianchi,
nel niente del costato.

***

Diranno: doveva capitare
qui, tra cari fantasmi,
tra specchi amari . . .
Ma se non uscivamo quasi mai,
se nemmeno aprivamo la finestra.

***

Lista di Spagna

But in Spain . . .
Don Giovanni, *Act I, Scene V*

The love
left there with paws
that are still moving, that would like
to run around, to climb up who knows where . . .

***

Thinking about your round
and sharp little face I was looking at Titian's
banners at the Frari.

***

The hyperbole that you love,
that you are: I adore you
in the curve of your hips,
in the nullity of your chest.

***

They'll say: it had to happen
here, amid beloved ghosts,
amid bitter mirrors . . .
But if we hardly ever went outside,
if we didn't even open up the window.

***

Il caffè non bevuto
aspettando il tuo sorgere di luna,
il tuo spavaldo, timido oscillare
sui tacchi, controluce.

***

Ah, le tue scollature: immaginare
la cosa che non pare,
la brusca, invisibile ascesa.

***

Inghiottita dal buio
la vecchia littorina che ti portava via
rimanevo sul posto a assaporare
la mia vista annebbiata, l'esultanza
del mio corpo stremato.

***

Una gioia di dopo, ancòra: chiuso,
solo, a sera, nel bozzolo
del nostro pomeriggio
fiutarti piano, a lungo sulla punta
delle mie dita.

***

E quella volta che ti sei truccata
da Veronica Lake, per farmi innamorare
anche da prima, da ragazzo — e io

The coffee left untouched
waiting for your moonrise,
your impudent, timid swaying
on heels, against the light.

***

Ah, your necklines: imagining
the unappearing thing,
the sudden, invisible rise.

***

The darkness swallowing
the old diesel train that carried you away
I stayed where I was to go on savoring
the view now clouded over, the exultation
of my exhausted body.

***

One joy of afterwards, still: closed in
alone, in the evening, in the cocoon
of our afternoon
tenderly scenting you for a long time on
my fingertips.

***

And that time you made yourself up to look
like Veronica Lake, to make me fall in love
even earlier, as a boy—and I

non me ne sono accorto, perso nel tuo profilo
di pupazzetto gotico . . .

***

No, non siamo cacciati
né cacciatori, amore mio — nessuno
di noi due. C'è qualcosa per il cuore.

***

Toccarti
dove sei dolce e umida mi dà
la sete che mi toglie,
mi guarisce e mi svena se ti fa,
dolcezza, umida appena . . .

***

Archi, un flauto, due oboi, due fagotti,
due corni in sol . . . tu vedi che ho l'ardire
di mettergli vicino la mia arcadia
povera, per ardore.

***

Nel bar pieno di gente
giovane che saluti e che mi guarda
come un intruso basta il tuo bisbiglio
docile e spudorato
— Vuoi che . . . ? — a farmi invisibile e beato.

***

didn't realize it, lost in your profile
of a little Gothic doll.

***

No, we are neither hunted
nor hunters, my love—neither
one of us. There's something for the heart.

***

Touching you
where you are sweet and moist gives me
the thirst that takes me, heals me
and opens my veins if it makes you,
my sweetness, slightly moist . . .

***

Strings, a flute, two oboes, two bassoons,
two horns in the key of G . . . you see I dare
to put them in the area of my poor
arcadia, out of ardor.

***

In a cafe full of young people
you say hello to and who look at me
as an intruder your mild and brazen whisper
"Would you like me to . . ." is all
it takes to make me blissful, invisible.

***

No, non ne ho avute mille e tre — nemmeno
seicento e quaranta, o novantuna.
E tu quanti? Di colpo, lunga o corta
che sia la lista, il cuore s'accartoccia,
fa male. Eppure so che non importa.

***

Che delizia sentirti raccontare
dei tuoi amori infantili e solitari,
del tuo darti piacere con l'immaginazione
e con le dita. Supplicavo invano
che me ne dessi una dimostrazione:
preferivi il mio cazzo, la mia mano.

***

Les feux d'une rousse chevelure,
sì, tesoro, lo so, non mi dà pace
questo Proust che non ami.
Ma come non amarlo se mi parla
di te lontana?

***

Nessuno per la strada, saltimbanco
o viandante. Vapori sul canale.
E tu che t'aggrappi al bottone
del mio loden, che vuoi portarlo via.

***

No, I haven't had a thousand and three—
not even six hundred and forty, or ninety-one.
And you, how many? Suddenly, no matter
how long or short the list is, the heart shrivels
and hurts. And yet I know it doesn't matter.

***

With what delight I heard you tell me of
all of your childish solitary loves,
of how you would pleasure yourself with imagination
and with your fingers. And then I was quick
to implore you to provide a demonstration,
in vain, for you preferred my hand, my prick.

***

Les feux d'une rousse chevelure,
Yes, love, he never gives me a moment's peace,
this Proust that you don't love.
But how can he not be loved if he speaks to me
of you so far away?

***

No one along the avenue, no jugglers
or people passing. Mists on the canal.
And you who hold on to the button of my loden,
who'd like to carry it away with you.

***

Una ghirlanda, un foglio per ciascuno
degli anni che volevi dimostrare,
che non avevi ancora,
che hai compiuti con me.

***

Sarò, m'annunciavi, vestita
da Zorro, pantaloni
strettissimi, mantello. O: Avrò le scarpe
bianche da Minnie, e forse una cintura
di vernice, alta e luccicante. Quante
stravaganti delizie
per pochi metri di strada,
fino al fulgore del tuo corpo nudo.

***

Chi la follia, chi l'alemanna . . . Il cuore
se do gioia e la prendo
nella tua fica
le danza tutte, amore.

***

Volevamo riempirci tutti i buchi,
io a te, tu a me, ricordi? dalle orecchie
ai meno nominabili.
Arrendersi era dolce, o rimandare.

***

A garland, and a page for every one
of the years that you wanted to show,
that you hadn't yet had,
that you turned with me.

***

I'll be, you announced to me, dressed,
as Zorro, in very tight
trousers, a cape. Or: I'll be wearing white
shoes like Minnie's, and a patent leather belt,
maybe, high and shiny. How many
extravagant delights
for a few feet of the street,
until the splendor of your naked body.

***

Some the folia, some the allemande . . . The heart,
if I give and take pleasure
in your cunt,
dances them all, my treasure.

***

We wanted to fill up all the holes we had,
I yours, you mine, remember? from the ears
to the least mentionable.
Surrendering was sweet, or postponing it.

***

Adoro i tuoi straccetti
neri, i tuoi veli, il sogno
che li ha sognati, il semplice
gesto con cui li togli.

***

È così nutriente, sai, l'ho letto
su un giornale, che forse
non l'avrei digerito . . .
E ti scusi, contrita, più adorabile
nel faccino devoto,
di non avermi deglutito, come
se avessi rifiutato
l'ultima parte della comunione.

***

Sei, mi dicevi, il mio riposo. E io
stavo immobile, zitto — imbalsamavo,
finto dormiente,
il tuo tenero sonno simulato.

***

Le nostre rade uscite
a notte fonda, cauti, perlustrando
ogni scorcio di calle, ogni cantone
di ponte . . . E sùbito la folla
che ci spintona, il biondo
che ti saluta, il mendicante cieco
che si volta a guardarti. È giorno pieno.

***

I adore your black rags,
your veils, the dream that
dreamt them, the simple movement
with which you take them off.

***

It's so nutritious, you know, I read it in
a newspaper, that I might not
have been able to digest it . . .
And you apologize, contrite, more adorable
in your devout little face,
for not having swallowed me,
as though you had
refused the last part of the communion.

***

You are, you told me, my repose. And I
stayed motionless and quiet– pretending to
be asleep, I embalmed
your tender simulated slumber.

***

Our rare excursions out
in the dead of night, cautiously exploring
the end of every alley and the corner
of every bridge . . . And suddenly the crowd
who jostle us, the blond man
who says hello to you, and the blind beggar
who turns to look at you. It's broad daylight.

***

Blanche fille aux cheveux roux, come tradurlo,
come tradurti? (e dire
che l'ho già fatto, tanto tempo fa . . .)
Ah mia bianca ragazza, mia candida puttana,
mia esangue ultima figlia,
bel muso infarinato, madonnina
della fortuna,
giglio di cera in una
grotta d'henné.

***

Vino dalla tua bocca, dolce tondo
dalla tua mano: voglio
quel sorso, quel pezzetto, non mi leva
sete né fame la memoria.

***

Se ti pettini in su, da giapponese
ti fai fiamminga — o viceversa? I nomi
cadono via, rimbalzano,
teste mozzate. Solo tu continui
un quarto dopo l'altro, mascherina
lucente,
sul tuo collo sottile.

(1981)

Blanche fille aux cheveux roux, how to translate it,
how to translate you? (and to think
that I've already done it, so long ago)
Ah my white girl, my spotless whore,
my pale last daughter,
pretty flour-covered mug, little madonna
of fortune,
wax lily in a
den of henna.

***

Wine from your mouth, sweet plate
from your hand: I want
that drop, that morsel, memory doesn't slake
my thirst or satisfy my hunger.

***

If you put up your hair, from Japanese
you turn Flemish—or vice versa? The names
fall away, they bounce,
severed heads. Only you go on
one quarter after another, shining little
mask,
on your slender neck.

(1981)

da A TANTO CARO SANGUE (1956–1987)

from WITH SUCH DEAR BLOOD (1956–1987)

I. Ultime (1983–1987)

I. Most Recent (1983–1987)

Dolore

Tu e le tue fissazioni! mi vien voglia
di rinfacciarti le mie piaghe,
quelle sì cancrenose, immedicabili . . .
Ma no, sbaglio. Non io, tu sei l'erede
d'una sacra penuria,
te e i tuoi da sempre ha saccheggiato il cielo.
C'è più tristezza nel tuo lutto
per un gioco perduto, per una bambola squartata
che nel mio per il novero dei morti
che colleziono da una vita.
È più giusta, ha più stoffa la tua pena.
E intanto non riesco a consolarti,
mio affamato, tremante, altero amore!
Non rispondi, mi guardi
come, ma sì, come un nemico di classe
se cerco di distrarti,
se ti ricatto con la tenerezza . . .
Ma credimi, tesoro, che non voglio rubartelo
l'osso del tuo dolore.

Pain

You and your fixations! the fancy takes me
to throw my lesions in your face,
incurable wounds, the ones gone gangrenous.
But no, I'm wrong. It's you, not I, who are heir
to a sacred scarcity,
heaven has always pillaged you and yours.
There's more sadness in your mourning
over a lost game, over a quartered doll
than in mine over the roster of the dead
I'm assembing in one life,
more justice and more substance in your grief.
And meanwhile I can't manage to console you,
my hungry, trembling, haughty love!
You don't respond, you look
at me, you do, as a class enemy
if I try to distract you,
if I blackmail you with tenderness . . .
But trust me, dear, I don't want to steal the bone
of your pain away from you.

Imbarcadero

I pochi che aspettano, pochi
per volta, pochi e sempre, che il traghetto
torni dall'altra riva
filando piatto, silenzioso
tranne i colpi da sotto, sordi,
dell'acqua scolorita
nel furioso nevischio di dicembre
e alla Salute, a San Tomà nessuno
che parli, solo uno
che si raschia la gola,
bestemmia, tende la mano all'obolo — oh diletti
vi ho ritrovati, vi ravviso
sotto ombrelli e cappucci, è il vostro corpo
stranamente visibile
che ancora migra, si riunisce
di là, dopo la terra,
a tanto caro sangue . . .

Landing

The few who are waiting, a few
at a time, a few and always, for the ferry
to return from the other bank
with oars flat, silent
except for the dull thuds from below
of the colorless water
in the furious sleet of December
and at Salute, at San Tomà no one
who says a word, only one
who clears his throat,
curses, holds out his hand for a coin—oh my darlings
I've found you again, I recognize you
under umbrellas and hoods, it's your strangely
visible bodies
that are still migrating, that reunite themselves
over there, after the earth,
with such dear blood . . .

La guerra

Ho gli anni di mio padre — ho le sue mani,
quasi: le dita specialmente, le unghie,
curve e un po' spesse, lunate (ma le mie
senza il marrone della nicotina)
quando, gualcito e impeccabile, viaggiava
su mitragliati treni e corriere
portando a noi tranquilli villeggianti
fuori tiro e stagione
nella sua bella borsa leggera
le strane provviste di quegli anni, formaggio fuso, marmellata
senza zucchero, pane senza lievito,
immagini della città oscura, della città sbranata
così dolci, ricordo, al nostro cuore.
Guardavamo ai suoi anni con spavento.
Dal sotto in su, dal basso della mia
secondogenitura, per le sue coronarie
mormoravo ogni tanto una preghiera.
Adesso, dopo tanto
che lui è entrato nel niente e gli divento
giorno dopo giorno fratello, fra non molto
fratello più grande, più sapiente, vorrei tanto sapere
se anche i miei figli, qualche volta, pregano per me.
Ma subito, contraddicendomi, mi dico
che no, che ci mancherebbe altro, che nessuno
meno di me ha viaggiato fra me e loro,
che quello che gli ho dato, che mangiare
era? non c'era cibo nel mio andarmene

The War

I am my father's age—I have his hands,
almost: his fingers especially, his nails,
curved, a bit thick, with crescent moons (but mine
without the chestnut-brown of nicotine)
when, rumpled and impeccable, he'd travel
on machine-gunned railway trains and buses
bringing in his handsome lightweight bag
to us placid vacationers
out of range and season
the strange provisions of those years, the processed cheese,
    unsweetened
marmalade, unleavened bread,
images of the darkened city, the shredded city,
that were, I recall, so precious to our hearts.
We thought about his age with apprehension.
Looking up from below, from the depth of my
secondogeniture, every now and then
I'd murmur a prayer for his coronary arteries.
Now, so long after
he's entered into nothingness and I
day by day am becoming his brother, soon to be
an older, wiser brother, I'd very much like to know
if my children also sometimes pray for me.
But right away, contradicting myself, I tell myself
that no, that would really be pushing it, that no one
has traveled less than I between me and them,
that in what I've given them, what nourishment
was there? There was no food in my clearing out

come un ladro e tornare a mani vuote . . .
Una povera guerra, piana e vile,
mi dico, la mia, così povera
d'ostinazione, d'obbedienza. E prego
che lascino perdere, che non per me
gli venga voglia di pregare.

like a thief and coming back with empty hands . . .
A poor war, easy and cowardly,
I tell myself, this one of mine, so poor
in persistence, in compliance. And I pray
that they let it go, that they have no
desire to pray for me.

Scongiuri vespertini

1

Fuori, nell'ora
dello zinco asciugato a cuore spento,
in timore di vento,
in contumacia di luna,
quando il tempo c'è e non c'è
e il canapo forza la cruna,
abbàssati il cappuccio,
fammi spavento se non ho paura,
resta con me
ora e nell'ora della tua fortuna.

2

« Tutto in ordine » cerco di pensare.
E invece ecco da crepe
riaffiorare nei muri
gli appuntamenti elusi, le promesse
non mantenute. Vorrei, corpo invisibile,
visitare i sepolcri e i lazzaretti
del passato, correggere, redimere.

Evening Invocations

1

Outside, at the hour when
the zinc counter is wiped down by the spent heart,
in dread of the wind,
in absentia of the moon,
when there is time and there is not
and the hawser forces the needle's eye,
let down your hood,
make me afraid if I have no fear,
stay with me
now and at the hour of your destiny.

2

"Everything in order," I'd like to think.
Yet I see from the cracks
reappearing in the walls
the appointments that were skipped, the promises
never kept. An invisible body, I would like
to visit the tombs and leprosariums
of times gone by, to correct and to redeem.

3

Nell'ombra dal telefono
pende una gelatina informe, un rettile
senza capo né coda. E con questo dovrei
raggiungere la voce del mio amore
lontano, lontano, nella parte boscosa
della città? Oh datemi un po' d'ali.
una gruccia, dei trampoli. Pietà.

4

L'arto amputato duole,
il naviglio interrato
intride di marcio le aiole.
Chiunque tu sia, monatto o gabelliere,
untore senza paga
o lancia mercenaria, non franare
nell'ellisse dei fari,
rinsàldati nel fumo che t'annera.

5

Adesso, ecco, guardando
questo povero cielo
dove il crepuscolo s'increspa appena, grigio
su grigio, grigio che striscia, che si sfibra nel grigio
stagno del mezzogiorno
mi cade goccia a goccia nelle vene
l'illusione soave
d'essere meglio che immortale

3

In the shadow of the telephone
dangles a shapeless gelatin, a reptile
with neither head nor tail. And with this thing
should I reach the voice of the one I love
far, far away from me in the wooded part
of the city? Oh let me have some wings,
a crutch, a pair of stilts. Pity.

4

The amputated limb still hurts,
the filled-in canal
soaks the flowerbeds with rot.
Whoever you are, corpse bearer or tax collector,
unpaid plague spreader
or mercenary lancer, don't collapse
in the headlights' ellipse,
solidify in the smoke that blackens you.

5

Now, here, beholding
this impoverished sky
where the twilight hardly ripples, gray
on gray, gray that slithers, fades and wears away
in the gray fen of midday
drop by drop there drips into my veins
the gentle illusion
of being better than immortal

perché ormai io lo so come si muore,
con che opaca dolcezza,
con che mite, domestico dolore . . .
O padre, padre tante volte
scongiurato a sproposito, ficcato
in tutte le salse delle mie seduzioni,
fa' che sia vero anche la volta vera
e che sia stato vero anche la volta
che si è rotto il tuo cuore.

because by now I know just how we die,
with what cloudy sweetness,
with what mild, domestic pain . . .
O father, father whom I would invoke in
folly so many times, stuck in
so many ways in my seductions,
make it be real as well in the real time
and make it have been real as well the time
when your heart was broken.

Codicilli

1

Pensavo
polvere, non cenere; non
arso, pensavo, né centrifugato;
polvere: e diventarlo
a poco a poco, a poco a poco sperdere
il duro delle ossa. E che la terra
non fosse poca né tanta,
né pesante né lieve a cancellare
lo scempio della fossa.
E che la terra fosse consacrata . . .
E che la terra fosse consacrata
e condivisa, lotto
numerato e introvabile
d'uno dei fiochi immensi cimiteri
che da nord, da nord-ovest
assediano Milano, che ci salvano,
barricate di croci,
d'angeli mutilati, dall'orrore
di marcire in privato, in un giardino.

2

Mangiarsi il capitale — strana, buffa espressione
di quando gente come me, borghese
per vizio o per condanna, s'ostinava

Codicils

1

I was thinking
dust, not ashes; not
burnt, I was thinking, not centrifuged;
dust, and turning into it
little by little, little by little dispersing
the hardness of the bones. And that the earth
would be neither a little nor a lot,
neither heavy nor light to obliterate
the massacre of the pit.
And that the earth would be consecrated . . .
And that the earth would be consecrated
and subdivided, a lot
numbered and undiscoverable
in one of those immense dim cemeteries
that from the north, from the northwest,
besiege Milan, that encircle and preserve us,
barricades of crosses,
of mutilated angels, from the horror
of rotting away in private, in a garden.

2

To consume your capital—a quaint, comical expression
that dates from a time when men like me, bourgeois
through defect or through sentencing, persisted

a vivere di rendita: una casa
in via Moscova, in via Boschetti, in via
San Primo (una dozzina
d'appartamenti solidi e un po' tetri, affittati
con giudizio) e nel ventre d'una banca,
sotto chiave, sotto ferro, qualche allegro mazzetto
di fogli colorati, obbligazioni
più o meno redimibili,
azioni al portatore . . .
Forse è così, ho vissuto
al di sopra dei miei mezzi,
ho sperperato i battiti del cuore,
ho intaccato la polpa. Ma che importa
se mi sono pagato la dolcezza
di vivere con te,
di morire, mia vita, accanto a te?

in living on unearned income: a house
in Via Moscova, in Via Boschetti, in Via
San Primo (a dozen
apartments, solid, a bit gloomy, sensibly
rented) and in the belly of a bank,
under lock and key, under iron, a bright little stack
of colored sheets, debentures
more or less redeemable,
shares payable to the bearer . . .
It may be so, I've lived
well beyond my means,
I've squandered many heartbeats,
I've drawn against the flesh. But what
does it matter if I've bought myself the sweetness
of living with you,
of dying here, my life, so close to you?

II. Disperse (1956–1960)

II. Uncollected (1956–1960)

Conversazione su niente

Un'altra idea poteva essere: parlarne
per qualche sera ancora, far finta
d'aver deciso, e alla fine rifiutare.
C'erano il pro e il contro, si capisce. (Su questo
tutti d'accordo.) Ai primi di gennaio
eravamo a questo punto, fiduciosi
nel tempo, un po' come il banditore quando aspetta
che la terza candela si consumi.

Conversation About Nothing

There could have been another idea: talking
about it for a few more evenings, pretending
a decision was made, and rejecting it in the end.
There were the pro and the con, you understand. (On this
all were agreed.) This was the point we'd reached
at the beginning of January, trusting
in time, just a little bit like the auctioneer when
he waits for the third candle to burn down.

L’estate nella villa in Brianza

L’estate nella villa in Brianza
con la nonna malata e i ritratti del nonno
morto nel ’29,
fa’ conto che sia di questo che ti parlo.
Una piena di scrupoli, a tacere
in alto, in fondo, dentro un cannocchiale
di stanze polverose;
l’altro in fuga per sempre, dallo studio
tenuto in mezzo lutto, dalla sala
dei vini secchi e del bigliardo . . .
Erano troppe due persone invisibili:
troppe per il ragazzo che filate
le preghiere, nel buio, credendo di vegliare
lottava con i mobili di noce.

Summer at the Villa in Brianza

Summer at the villa in Brianza
with a sick grandmother and portraits of a grandfather
who died in '29,
suppose that's what I'm telling you about.
One of them very scrupulous, keeping mum
up high, down low, inside a telescope
of dusty rooms;
the other one in flight forever, from
the study maintained in half mourning, from
the room of billiards and dry wines . . .
They were two too many invisible presences:
too many for the boy who, spinning out
his prayers, in the dark, thinking to keep watch,
struggled with the walnut furniture.

Interno esterno

La poltrona di faggio e canna d'India
lasciata a dondolare
tra pianoforte verticale e muro,
la brace che si vede e non si vede
nel suo povero loculo di ghisa
e fuori ripide le scale, nera
la balaustra, greve
la nebbia in questo grumo
di stradine, Laghetto, Pasquirolo,
pressi della croce del Verziere dove
han già messo gli antoni alle botteghe
e se c'è ancora un po' di luce viene
da bottiglierie livide, fumose
di questurini in borghese
intenti a fingersi intenti
al tressette, al calice, alle grazie sfiorite
della padrona
lentamente si ferma, lentamente
si spegne.

Interior Exterior

The armchair made of reed and Indian cane
left there to swing
between the upright piano and the wall,
the embers that you see and that you don't see
inside their poor cast-iron burial niche
and outside the staircase steep, the banister
black, the fog
heavy in this clump
of tiny streets, Laghetto, Pasquirolo,
close to the cross of the Verziere where
they've already drawn the gates of the little shops
and if there's still a bit of light it comes
from the smoky and colorless cantinas
with cops in plain clothes
intent on trying to look intent
on *tressette*, on a glass, on the faded charms
of the proprietress
slowly it ceases, slowly
they go out.

Gli addii

Ogni tanto mi sforzo
di ricordarli: il ladro di verdura,
il matto, la servante au grand coeur,
il medico ecc. Strano gioco,
ho paura, e assai poco redditizio.
Tanto tempo è passato! e io
che mi gratto la testa e sto seduto
al tavolo di pietra del mulino
aspettando il sereno, non
sento di quelle spente dolcezze più
che un rauco, degradato miagolio.

The Farewells

Every once in a while
I try to recall them all, the vegetable thief,
the madman, and *la servante au grand coeur*,
the physician, etc. A curious game,
I fear, and one that's quite unprofitable.
How much time has gone by! and I
who scratch my head and go on sitting here
at the stone table of the mill
waiting for the sky to clear,
all that I still hear now of those faded joys
is the noise of a degraded, shrill meow.

da VERSI GUERRIERI E AMOROSI (1984–1989)

from VERSES OF WAR AND LOVE (1984–1989)

Per una ragione improvvisa la luce si è fatta bianca e fissa: i passanti, smilzi e sbigottiti come se avessero in testa un gibus o una magiostrina, hanno smesso di colpo di fare ombra; nella facciata del teatro non si vede una sola crepa. Sono passati quarantaquattro anni, un mese e un giorno. Non è passato neanche un minuto. Mio padre, elegante e asciutto come un ufficiale di legno traforato, è appena salito sull'1 dalla porta anteriore riservata agli abbonati e probabilmente agli invalidi esibendo al manovratore la sua tessera valida per l'intera rete tranviaria. Impossibile, in tutto questo bianco, non accorgersi che la vettura è verde. Invece nessuno se ne accorge, perché tutti i tram e tutti i tassì sono verdi e non è ragionevole né decente supporre che un giorno, un giorno di questo stesso secolo, potranno non esserlo più.

Mio padre sale dalla porta anteriore, vietata ai non abbonati e ai non ancora invalidi, su una vettura della linea tranviaria numero 1. Come di consueto, non è né in ritardo né in anticipo. Fra due fermate le portiere del tram, aprendosi, sfioreranno le foglie dei platani della piazza. Fra tre anni, un mese e ventisette giorni non ci saranno più platani. Mio padre, che in tram non si siede mai, si regge a una maniglia di cuoio e non vede i platani (né potrebbe notare la loro assenza) perché guarda, come di consueto, dall'altra parte.

Fra quattro fermate, il tram arriverà ai grattacieli. La luce è sempre più bianca e fissa. Mancano tre fermate. Mancano dodici minuti e diciannove secondi. Mancano quattro anni, dieci mesi e quindici giorni, un metro e trentasei centimetri di neve, un numero imprecisabile di mitragliamenti a bassa quota. Mancano ventisette gradini. In casa, nella penombra del cortile, una mano sta già toccando la manopola di bachelite della radio.

For an unforeseen reason the light has become white and steady: the passersby, spare and dismayed as if they were wearing top hats or straw hats, have suddenly ceased casting shadows; in the façade of the theater there's not a single crack to be seen. Forty-four years, one month and one day have passed. Not even one minute has passed. My father, elegant and lean as a fretworked wooden officer, has just boarded the No. 1 by the forward door reserved for passholders and probably for invalids, showing the driver his pass good for the entire streetcar system. Impossible, in all this whiteness, not to notice that the car is green. On the contrary, no one notices it, because all the streetcars and taxis are green and it's neither reasonable nor proper to imagine that one day, one day in this very century, they might not be green anymore.

My father boards by the forward door, forbidden to nonpassholders and to those who are not yet invalids, of a car on the No. 1 line. As is his habit, he's neither late nor early. Within two stops the streetcar's doors, as they open, will be grazing the leaves of the plane trees in the square. Within three years, one month and twenty-seven days the plane trees will be gone. My father, who never sits down on the streetcar, stands holding a leather strap and doesn't see the plane trees (nor could he take note of their absence) because he is looking, as is his habit, out the other side.

Within four stops, the streetcar will arrive at the skyscrapers. The light is whiter and whiter, steadier and steadier. There are three stops to go. There are twelve minutes and nineteen seconds to go. There are four years, ten months and fifteen days, four feet and four and a half inches of snow, an indeterminable number of low-altitude bursts of machine-gun fire to go. There are twenty-seven steps to go. At home, in the semidarkness of the courtyard, a hand is already touching the bakelite knob of the radio.

Dà dolore e insieme vergogna
il piccolo male un po' santo
che per freddo (ma non soltanto)
tormenta le dita e il calcagno,

i geloni dico, al ragazzo
spaurito dati in abbondanza
scagliandolo nell'alternanza
di pena furore e imbarazzo

e in così fiera e fatua danza
rendendo anzitempo più fioco
il suo cuore a questo gioco
arrischiava la sua fragranza

senza sapere che fra poco
o tanto, ma allora era vano
e adesso è tardi, la tua mano
corroderà lo stesso fuoco.

With shame and suffering intermixed,
the little affliction a bit holy
working through cold (but not cold only)
torments the heels and fingertips,

I mean the chilbains, a murrain
to scare a boy out of his wits
inflicting alternating fits
of rage, embarrassment, and pain

and in so hollow and hot a dance
weakened the heart before its time
whose fragrance he put on the line
in this very game of chance

before he'd begun to understand
how soon or much, although then vain
and late now, that this selfsame flame
will be eroded by your hand.

Non facevano fumo né rumore
nei piazzali ghiacciati le corriere
degli sfollati in quelle bianche sere
di prima guerra e d'antico dolore

fagocitando e cancellando a schiere
i silenziosi corpi traghettanti
e negando anche il suono ai mille pianti
pagati all'invisibile nocchiere

finché infine in un tempo che non fa
mestiere d'abbandoni e di tormenti
sia il colore che l'audio non inventi
il marchingegno della tua pietà.

With neither smoke nor noise the coaches bore
loads of evacuees across the ice
that lined the open squares on those white nights
of ancient misery and the first war

phagocytizing and erasing then
the piles of silent corpses they conveyed
negating even the sound of the tears paid
in thousands to the invisible steersman

until at last in a time that doesn't know
a need for torments and abandonments
the contraption of your sympathy invents
the color picture and the audio.

Dal fuoco stinto dei nespoli sale
l'ansia di una remota eucarestia
respinta in petto ma non nella mia
gola tremando senza confessione

quasi che l'incertezza fosse il male
cui non vale rimedio né perdono
e acqua e farina tramite d'ustione
del più orribile grado che ci sia

all'atterrito esofago che solo
con te, mia acqua, e ben tardi consolo.

There rises from the medlars' faded flame
the anxiety of a distant eucharist
that I rejected in my breast but not
in my trembling throat (for I had not confessed)

as though my doubting were the sin and shame
with no forgiveness and no remedy
and water and flour the way to a fire as hot
and horrible as any there could be

to the terror-stricken gullet I palliate
only with you, my water, and so late.

Sì, ricordo: chi viene dalla notte
ha il suo segno di luce, vivo o spento,
cerchio ovale o losanga, e il suo lamento
o il suo silenzio nelle appena rotte

tenebre della strada. Ma non sento
se era a dinamo o a pila la tua spora,
anima, quando non essendo ancora
mi sfioravi nel buio come un vento.

Yes, I remember: all of those who come
from the night have their sign of light, alive or spent,
circle oval or diamond, and their lament
or their silence in the barely broken gloom

of the street. But I can't tell if a battery's
or a dynamo's charge had energized your spore,
my soul, when in the darkness, even before
you were a being, you grazed me like a breeze.

Adorammo le scorte
segrete, il variopinto
scatolame murato
nei vani delle porte,

il latte condensato
sepolto fra le morte
corde del pianoforte,
i vasetti d'estratto

Liebig nel catafratto
vuoto dell'impiantito,
testimoni allibiti
d'un appetito estinto

per fame cui sorella
specularmente è quella
che non accesa brilla
luce della tua stella.

How we adored the stores
of secret stash, the bold-
colored canned goods walled
in the hollows of the doors,

powdered milk tins packed
in amid dead wires
of the piano, all the jars
of Liebig beef extract

hidden in the floor's
empty catafract,
astonished witnesses
to an appetite extinct

out of hunger whose
sister specularly
is that unignited she,
your star that brightly glows.

La preghiera ansimante per connubi
d'apprensione e di sonno nell'oltraggio
dei vetri sconquassati dal passaggio
di fortezze volanti oltre le nubi

fatte candore anzi smeriglio al raggio
obliquo e muto della contraerea
ma cruente più in là dove l'eterea
notte si muta in crepitante ostaggio

giungerà all'amen quando con la vita
finirà la paura che il coraggio
finisca prima che abbia fine il viaggio
e la tua latitanza sia finita.

Prayer panting in the marrying of frightened
waiting and of sleeping in the outrage
of windows smashed to splinters by the passage
of flying fortresses above clouds whitened

and even roughened in the silent vantage
of anti-aircraft's slanting beam of light
but bloody later where the ethereal night
turns further on into a sputtering hostage

will come to its amen when life is done
and with its ending ends the fear that courage
will end before the ending of the voyage
and ended is your being on the run.

Che gioia nominarle ignote e già
familiari per tipo e tonnellaggio
immobili allo sbarco o ancora in viaggio
per la costa normanna le unità

navali traghettanti libertà
su questa amara trepidante riva
d'Europa! Come il mare, si gremiva
di futuro la fosca verità.

Eppure, vedi, ma vittoria fu
così vana o più forte la deriva.
Con la dolcezza di saperti viva
tutto rivive tranne la virtù.

What joy to name the unknown and previously
familiar by class and tonnage already lying
at anchor for the landing or still plying
their way to reach the coast of Normandy

the naval vessels ferrying liberty
onto this harsh and apprehensive shore
of Europe! And with all the ships of war
the future's dark truth rushed in, like the sea.

And yet, you see, there never was before
so strong a drift, so vain a victory.
In the sweetness of knowing yourself to be
alive, all but virtue revives once more.

da OGNI TERZO PENSIERO (1989–1993)

from EVERY THIRD THOUGHT (1989–1993)

Ombra ferita, anima che vieni
zoppicando, strisciando dal tuo fioco
asilo a cercare nei sogni il poco
che rosicchio per te all'andirivieni

dei risvegli e degli incubi, agli osceni
cortei delle sciarade, così poco
che qualche volta quando arrivi il fuoco
è già spento, divelte le imposte, pieni

di insulsi intrusi o infidi replicanti
l'immensità della cucina, il banco
di scuola, il letto, dammi tempo, non

svanire, il tempo di chiudere i tanti
conti vergognosi in sospeso con
loro prima di stendermi al tuo fianco.

Wounded shadow, spirit with your slow
and halting movements, creeping now from your
dim shelter, here to find in dreams the poor
little bit I gnaw for you in the to and fro

of awakenings and nightmares, in the show
of charades' obscene processionals, so poor
that there are times that you come to my door
to find the shutters torn away and no

fire, the vastness of kitchen, school desk, bed
all filled up with insipid intruders or
perfidious replicants, give me some time, do

not vanish, give me time to close instead
so many shameful accounts with them before
I lie down and am stretched out next to you.

Sonetti di infermità e convalescenza

Sonnets of Illness and Convalescence

Il vuoto non manca,
lo attesta il sapiente
d'Irlanda alla mente
che si sfiata e stanca

in cerca del niente
per finire bianca
di paura e stanca
da morire in niente

lei stessa, una palpebra
che stringersi illude
che è notte ma intorno

latitante il giorno
non apre né chiude
l'orrore che celebra.

No lack of void, our friend
the Irish sage makes clear
to the mind that's left
tired and out of breath

seeking nothing, in the end
to turn white with fear
and tired unto death
in nothingness itself,

when an eyelid's shut
quite tight it simulates
the dark of nighttime, but

all around absconding day
neither shows nor hides away
the horror it celebrates.

L'ordine di non avere
un solo pelo più in basso
del mento fa come un sasso
raccolto al mare o la cera

d'un santo in un buio basso
lividamente a giacere
sotto vetro fra preghiere
il corpo che a passo a passo

liberato sul più bello
dall'odiosa sincronia
di percezione ed evento

per l'interporsi del lento
flap della preanestesia
va spensierato al macello.

The order that there not be
any hair below the chin
means soon it will begin
to seem a stone from the sea

or the wax of a saint glassed in
low dark lying lividly
mid prayers, this body set free
at just the right time and then

liberated step by step
from the odious synchrony
of perception and event

by intruding the slow flap
of pre-anesthesia and sent
to the slaughterhouse worry-free.

Sul fievole tormento
di dormire supino
veglia da un altarino
elettronico il lento

ammiccante lumino
del macchinario intento
a sedare il tormento
d'un disastro intestino

nell'attesa che il muro
inalberi il pallore
dell'alba e da un impuro

sogno riemerso il cuore
ricacci nel futuro
l'ansia del disonore.

From a small electronic shrine
in the darkness a nocturnal
light that is slowly flashing
on machinery for assuaging

the torment of an internal
catastrophe maintains
a vigil over the faint
torment of sleeping supine

in the wait for the wall to raise
dawn's pallor and the heart
as it re-emerges from

an impure dream to start
pushing off till days to come
the anxiety of disgrace.

Nel decomporsi chissà
che rumore fa il cervello
e che scintille se già
così assordante è il rovello

d'essere, ecco, la metà
dell'annegato, il fratello
siamese di chi non ha
più volto nel mulinello

insieme a precipizio vivi
travolti da un'atassia
divina e a un divino niente

centuplicata la mente
flottando morti nella scia
fulgida dei sedativi.

Who knows what noise comes out
of the brain as it decomposes
and what sparks it produces
deaf from the nagging thought

of being, say, half of another,
the drowned Siamese twin
whose face is already gone,
swept away alive together

headlong in the whirling lake
by a divine ataxia, mind
multiplied a hundred times

to a divine oblivion
then dead and floating in
the sedatives' dazzling wake.

Ah no, non a un filo soltanto
era attaccata la mia vita
ma al buffo intrico ch'era vanto
dell'infermiera vietnamita

e goccia dopo goccia intanto
che pareggiava la partita
del molto sangue dentro sparso
per delega della ferita

di taglio e punta a un altro male
così silenzioso che anch'io
fui quasi per crederlo un bene

versava in più nelle mie vene
il cocktail di plasma e d'oblio
d'una triaca trionfale.

No, it wasn't just a thread
life hung by, but one of these
comic tangles by my bed,
pride of my Vietnamese

nurse, that splash by splash
dripped silently till it tied
the blood I had lost inside
by decree of incision's slash

and another ailment's sting,
so quietly I had begun
almost thinking it a good thing,

the cocktail in its sack,
plasma mixed with oblivion
of a triumphal theriac.

Il faut être très précis
avec les urines, parola
senza incertezze, la sola
che abbia ancora corso qui

e comandando consola
la mente e il cuore di chi
per più dolcezze smarrì
la dolcezza della scuola

con l'estatico dovere
di collezionarsi, ora
dopo ora, via decilitri,

via litri in torbidi vetri
dove un ammanco che ignora
colma il rene fabbriciere.

Il faut être très précis
avec les urines: a clear
word, the only one here
that still has currency

and commanding now consoles
his mind and heart, who for
more sweets had lost his school's
sweetness, with the ecstatic

task of being gathered
hour by hour in murky
glass tubes in liters all

the while that the hardworking
kidney makes up a shortfall
of which it's unaware.

Avvinta la vita a pochi
grumi vegetali inventa
di svanire da una spenta
veglia ai rapinosi giochi

notturni ove rappresenta
sé a sé tra gli opposti fuochi
del desiderio e ai più fiochi
fantasmi sùbito attenta

non si stupisce che stia
nel prima il dopo, nel padre
il figlio e perdutamente

così ha memoria del niente
da smemorarsi che arde
nel suo polso l'anemia.

Life, attached only slightly
to vegetable clumps, is making
an exit from weary waking,
contriving to play nightly

ravishing games to portray
itself to itself in opposed
flames of desire, and pay
quick heed to more faded ghosts,

is unamazed that first
holds last, that father contains
son, and so passionately

holds nothing in memory
to forget the burning burst
of anemia in the veins.

Pullulava di sergenti
più o meno loschi il mattino
ma soavi a porgere un lino
sine macula ai tormenti

in cui si crogiola fino
a che s'accordino a lenti
lucori i trasalimenti
del suo cuore l'inquilino

immaginario del mio
letto, lui sì non invano
solvente se un sogno schiude

la porta, quella!, fra nude
pareti entra un capitano
with drum and colours e addio.

Morning swarmed with more or less
shady sergeants, who gently provide
sine macula linen to tide
him over in the distress

he simmers in till they've addressed
his spikings, till palpitations
drop to slow illuminations,
the imaginary paying guest

in my bed, and it's quite certain
he's not solvent in vain should it happen
a door's opened up by a dream,

that one right there!, and between
the bare walls in comes a captain
with drum and colours and curtain.

Niente comporta le delizie
del pasto d'un riabilitato
a vivere appena svezzato
dalle protettive nequizie

dei fili e nuovamente in stato
eretto ai cautelosi sfizi
restituito (e bei palmizi
fuori) del prosciutto tritato

fine, del soffice purè,
della pasta soavemente
scotta soprattutto se c'è

così paziente non paziente
nella stanza quattro per tre
la fiera nemica del niente.

Nothing kills a meal's delights
for one rehabilitated
to living, just liberated,
weaned from protective blights

of wires and newly erect,
restored to joy by degrees
(and to the lovely palm trees
outside) with a just overcooked

pasta, a finely minced ham,
a mild purée, particularly
if in the ten-by-twelve room

so patient and nonetheless so
impatient there also is she,
of nothing the fierce and proud foe.

Altri sonetti

Other Sonnets

Preghiere per i morti — tutta qui
la mia fede? So solo che ogni sera,
così rispondo, aguzzo la mia povera
vista nel buio per scoprire chi

più m'aspetta, chi mi fa cenno di
là d'un'asciutta e tersa primavera
del '40, '41 all'austera
ombra dei platani e se e come io lì

potrò col mio corpo risorgere, ombra
protettiva e tremante fra le care
tre ombre così intente a conversare

che né l'erbaccia che il giardino ingombra
né la luce ormai presta a declinare
fa per loro le dalie meno chiare.

Prayers for the dead—is my whole faith right here?
I only know that I respond each night
in just this way, I focus my poor sight
into the darkness as I strain to peer

and see who still awaits, who beckons me
from over there, a springtime dry and clear
in '40, '41 in the austere
shadow of plane trees and if it can be,

and how, that with my body I may rise
again, a trembling and protective shade
with three dear shadows so intent on talking

that neither the weedy garden where we're walking
nor the light that will soon begin to fade
can make the dahlias dimmer in their eyes.

Niente può rovinarmela la festa
del mattino, quando il sole che dà
fiato alla sua raucedine ridesta
a dolori e crimini la città

che amo e nel cuore la felicità
d'esserle ancora complice. S'arresta
a questo confine la potestà
di numeri e fantasmi, qui la cresta

sbrindellata alza la vita e tace
l'arcangelo del rimorso. È la luce
la mia morfina. Su, mi dico, datti

da fare, mostra di che sei capace,
ficca mani e naso dove riluce
come un tesoro l'ovvietà dei fatti.

Nothing can spoil for me the festival
of morning, when the sun that gives its rough
throat breath begins to rouse the city full
of griefs and crimes, the city that I love,

and rouse in my heart the happiness to still
be its accomplice. Here there is nothing of
numbers or ghosts, all of their power null
and void at this boundary, while up above

life hoists its tattered crest, with no syllable
from the archangel of remorse. The light
is my morphine. It's time to act, I tell

myself, up now and show what you can do,
thrust your hands and nose where treasure-bright
the obviousness of facts lights up anew.

Senza desideri, senza speranze
che si potesse vivere, una volta
non riuscivo a crederci. Adesso, molta
vita dopo, mi domando se anzi

non sia così, dai già funebri avanzi
di quelli e di quelle una buona volta
come da una placenta o un guscio sciolta,
che la mente (l'anima) un po' più avanza

nella gioia . . . e pensandosi sostanza
che pensa e nomina sé e ogni cosa
senza rimpianti assapora la storia

d'ogni istante, d'ogni salmo la gloria,
polvere prodigiosa che si posa
sulle fioche reliquie della danza.

No hopes and no desires: I'd have said
at one time I could not imagine how
it was possible to live that way. But now
I wonder, much life later, if instead,

set free forever from the already dead
remains of hope and of desire as well
as if from a placenta or a shell,
the mind (the spirit) takes a step ahead

in happiness . . . and thinking itself the core
that thinks and names itself and every thing
proceeds with no regrets to savoring

the story of every moment and the glory
of every psalm, prodigious dust that lands
and settles on faint relics of the dance.

Sono quello che eravate, sarò
quello che siete, sussurro a chi spia
i miei passi da un letto di corsia
d'un padiglione di Niguarda o

del vecchio policlinico di via
Sforza, mi sopravalutate, ho
un rene solo, presto perderò
l'ultima battaglia con la miopia

e il cuore, eh, il cuore . . . No, perdono, care
anime, perdono! non posso fare
l'unto della Morte qui, non si deve

insegnare a morire a chi già tanto
muore e così poco spera, soltanto
un'altra primavera, un'altra neve.

I'm what you were, it won't be long before
I'm what you are, I murmur to anyone
who spies me walking by from a bed upon
the ward of the Niguarda pavilion or

the hall of the old polyclinic on
the Via Sforza, you credit me with more
than I deserve, soon I will lose my war
with myopia, now I have only one

kidney, and oh the heart, the heart . . . But no,
dear souls, I beg your pardon, I cannot
play Death's anointed here, nobody ought

to teach the art of dying to those who
are dying so much already, whose hopes are few,
only another spring, another snow.

Invecchiando il corpo vorrebbe un'anima
diversa, ma come si fa? non serve
prendere calmanti, stordire i nervi
e la mente, il problema è proprio l'anima,

l'anima che non vuole pace, l'anima
insaziabile, ostinata che ferve
per sempre più comicamente impervi
labirinti o abissi e si sa che l'anima

non solo è immortale ma immortalmente
immatura. Così, temo, non resta
che rassegnarsi, finché non s'arresta

la fontanella del respiro niente
può cambiare, non è di questo fuoco
spegnersi come gli altri a poco a poco.

The aging body wants a different soul
but what can be done for it? It hardly serves
to swallow sedatives, to numb the nerves
and brain, the problem really is the soul,

the soul that wants no peace, the stubborn soul
insatiable in its burning swoops and swerves
through ever more laughably difficult drops and curves
in chasms or labyrinths, and we know the soul

is not just immortal but immortally
immature. I'm afraid there's no help for it,
the only thing to do is to submit,

till the stream of breath dries up it'll never be
any different, for as long as this flame's still lit
it doesn't die out like others bit by bit.

Non sono bandiere queste bandiere,
vedi che invece di ferite e ustioni
hanno fiori alle finestre, ai balconi
le case. Da infinite primavere

la giostra, qui, s'è fermata, i padroni
l'hanno portata altrove. Ma di sere
così, di notti come quelle, nere
fino all'occlusione, marce di tuoni,

tu sai che affanno e con che artigli preme
il semplice cuore. La verità
è che nessuna guerra è mai finita,

che la stessissima ferita geme
per sempre, che solo chi non ne ha
può scacciare i ricordi dalla vita.

They aren't flags, these flags, you can see how
instead of having burns and injuries
the houses have flowers on their balconies,
in windows. And for endless springtimes now

the carousel, here, has been stopped, brought by
the owners to some other place. Yet still
on evenings and on nights like those, black till
the occlusion, nights when thunder rots the sky,

you know what worry, with what talons, takes
hold of the simple heart. And, truth to tell,
there's never any end to any war,

and it's the same wound that forever aches,
and only those without it can dispel
memories of the way things really are.

Sì, certo, sarebbe bello abitare
dove una vera guerra non c'è stata,
una città intatta, né bombardata
né ricostruita, da conquistare

un poco ogni giorno nella passata
sua gloria finché sconfitto scompare
ogni fantasma del presente e chiare
come un tempo alla mente non turbata

si fanno le voci dei morti. Uguale
sorte però non avrebbero, inutile
farsi illusioni, i sogni, se non vale

altro passato a mutarli, se sono
passato già essi, e in più presente, in mutile
e reciproche attese di perdono.

Yes, certainly, it would be beautiful
to live in a city that has never seen
real war, an undamaged city that's never been
bombarded and rebuilt, to feel its pull

and a little bit each day to be drawn in
and conquered by its glorious past until
we rout the ghosts of the present day and still
clear as before to the mind at peace begin

hearing voices of the dead. But, anyway,
they wouldn't have the selfsame destiny,
useless to raise illusions, dreams, if they

wouldn't be changed by another past, if they're past
yet somehow still present, mutilated, reciprocally
waiting until forgiveness comes at last.

da QUARE TRISTIS (1998)

from QUARE TRISTIS (1998)

Tanto difficile da immaginare,
davvero, il paradiso? Ma se basta
chiudere gli occhi per vederlo, sta
lì dietro, dietro le palpebre, pare

che aspetti noi, noi e nessun altro, festa
mattutina, gloria crepuscolare
sulla città invulnerata, sul mare
di prima della diaspora — e si desta

allora, non la senti? una lontana
voce, lontana e più vicina come
se non l'orecchio ne vibrasse ma

un altro labirinto, una membrana
segreta, tesa nel buio a metà
fra il niente e il cuore, fra il silenzio e il nome . . .

Is it so hard to imagine paradise
after all? If all you really need to do
is close your eyes to see it, it stays for you
behind your lids, and seemingly it lies

waiting for us, for us, for no one but us two,
dawn feast and twilight glory in the skies
above the unwounded city, above the blue
and prediasporan sea—don't you hear the rise

of a distant voice that sounds as if it came
from far away yet somehow very near
as if vibrating not inside the ear

but another labyrinth, a secret, unseen
membrane in the dark halfway between
the nothing and the heart, the silence and the name . . .

Niente sarà mai vero come è
vero questo venticinque dicembre
millenovecentonovantatré
con il suo tranquillo traffico d'ombre

per corsie e sale e camerate ingombre
di vuoto e il fiume dei ricordi che
rompe gli argini in silenzio. È in novembre,
lo so, vuoi che non lo sappia? per te

che si semina dolore, il più forte,
il più contro la vita — ma se viene
solo ora al suo compimento di morte

e di lì a un'altra nascita conviene
far festa qui, bruciare qui le scorte
di incenso e febbre al turno delle pene.

Nothing will ever be as real to me
as is this twenty-fifth day of December
in the year nineteenhundredninetythree
with its calm flow of shadows without number

into where halls and wards and sickrooms slumber
cluttered with emptiness and the silently
cresting river of memories. It's in November,
I know (but do you wish I didn't see?),

that sorrow is sown for you, the most severe
and anti-life—and yet if it has come
only now to be fulfilled in death and from

there to another birth, the better thing
is to live it up, burn stores of incense here
and fever at our turn for suffering.

« Caduto in A. O. », certo, perché no?
Non soltanto da Auschwitz, da Hiroshima,
dall'Indocina, comincia da prima
la conta dei pogrom, il borderò

dei massacri che attraversa da cima
a fondo quel po' di vita che so
d'aver vissuto, quel tanto che ho
sperperato cercando di far rima

con tutte le parole della terra . . .
Che strida nella sua Patmo Giovanni
ha udito, di quante stragi si tace

nel suo cuore . . . E pensare che la guerra
è finita che avevo tredici anni,
poi c'è stata, lo sappiamo, la pace.

"Fallen in Africa," sure, why wouldn't he be?
Not just at Auschwitz, Hiroshima, or
in Indochina: it begins before,
the reckoning of pogroms, the registry

of massacres from the ceiling to the floor
of that bit of life that I can certainly
say that I've lived, the great majority
of which I've thrown away in looking for

the rhymes for all the words the world can hold . . .
What cries he's heard, Saint John upon the shore
of Patmos, from the slaughters he keeps close,

silent within his heart . . . And to think the war
was over when I was thirteen years old,
and then came peace, as everybody knows.

Stare coi morti, preferire i morti
ai vivi, che indecenza! Acqua passata.
Vedo che adesso più nessuno fiata
per spiegarci gli osceni rischi e torti

dell'assenza, adesso che è sprofondata
la storia . . . E così tocca a noi, ci importi
tanto o quel tanto, siano fiochi o forti
i mesti richiami dell'ostinata

coscienza, alzare questa poca voce
contro il silenzio infinitesimale
a contestare l'infinito, atroce

scempio dell'esistente . . . (Al capitale
forse è questo che può restare in gola,
l'osso senza carne della parola.)

To spend time with the dead, preferring these
over the living, what indecency!
Spilt milk. Nobody bothers now, I see,
to explain to us the obscene injuries

and risks of absence, now that history's
collapsed . . . It's up to us, to what degree
it matters to us, however forcefully
or feebly come the melancholy pleas

of obstinate conscience, to lift up a small
voice against the infinitesimal
silence, to challenge the heinous, infinite

destruction of the existing . . . (And after all
perhaps this fleshless bone of the word is it,
the thing that will stick in the throat of capital.)

Filare tra le lenzuola tremando
di febbre, di felicità al pensiero
d'essere esente dall'esserci, libero
dal suo fiato, dal suo affanno — ma quando?

solo ai tempi dei tempi, quando ero
un ragazzo e proprio così, sfumando
il presente e il futuro in un rimando
sine die ne facevo più leggero

il morso? O forse la si prende, questa
malattia, anche da grandi, e forse è grazia
che sia così, grazia per chi s'appresta

a lasciare la vita e ancora strazia
il moto che la consuma, l'impura
dolcezza che la feconda e l'oscura.

Scooting between the sheets and shivering in
fever, in pleasure to think how it would be
to be exempt from being there, and free
from its breath and from its breathlessness—but when?

only in times long gone, back when I was
a boy and really a boy, pushing away
present and future, adjourning *sine die*,
trying to make the sting of them seem less

severe? Or perhaps it's catching, this disease,
even when we're adults, perhaps a blessing,
a blessing for one preparing to take leave

of life, though still tormented by the pressing
motion consuming it, the maculate
sweetness that fecundates and darkens it.

Fra l'Anschluss e la notte dei cristalli,
fra Monaco e Danzica li potrei
collocare con precisione quei
pochi giorni d'ecumene, di balli

senza fantasmi, quando tutti i miei
mai assenti eran presenti, vassalli
dell'aria e del sole negli intervalli
del sogno della morte . . . Ma ne sei

proprio sicuro? e allora quella gita
fuori porta, fuori dazio, guidata
da lui, dal primo a sparire, Caronte

di se stesso, scheletrito al volante
dell'ultima, più chiara, più cromata
decappottabile della sua vita?

Between the Anschluss and the Kristallnacht,
between Munich and Danzig I could place
precisely in that period those few days
of *ecuméne*, when the dances lacked

phantoms, days when all my people who
are never absent were truly present, there
as vassals of the sunlight and the air
in the intervals of the dream of death . . . Are you

really certain of it, though? and then that drive
past city gates and tollhouse, far from home,
led by the first to disappear, his own

Charon, nothing then but skin and bone
at the wheel of the last, the shiniest, most chrome-
decorated convertible of his whole life?

« Digli qualcosa, pensa che è venuto
solo per te » sentivo in un bisbiglio
dirgli qualcuno. Ma se ero io
a essere, da quando ero lì, muto

non sapendo chi di noi due era il figlio,
chi domandava e chi negava aiuto,
chi era la copia, il sosia, il sostituto
dell'altro . . . Che strano, buffo scompiglio

in quella stanza sul cortile dove
siamo morti un po' tutti, prima uno
poi l'altra e poi chissà e non sai se piove

o nevica, se è ancora il '51
o è già il '53, se il sogno è dove
ci siamo tutti o non c'è più nessuno.

“Tell him something, he thinks that he is here
only for you,” I heard somebody else
tell him, whispering. But if it was myself
who was silent since I’d been there, and unclear

which of us two was the son, which of us was
requesting and which of us refusing help,
which was the double, substitute, second self
of the other . . . What a strange, ridiculous

confusion in that room on the courtyard where
we all died a bit, first one, then the other one,
then who knows and you don’t know if it’s rain

or snow out there, if it’s still ’51
or already ’53, if the dream is where
we’re all together or there’s no one there.

Poi lo vorrò per me quello che voglio
per quei cari — un'infinita, quieta
attesa della quiete. La vieta
a chi vive, lo so bene, l'orgoglio

d'essere ancora vivo: me ne spoglio
con calma, ogni giorno un po', non c'è meta
più certa, né trama meno segreta
se è scritta da chissà quando nel foglio

su cui scrivo, nella bibbia contesa
al macero o alla fiamma. Ma tu intanto,
ti prego, sopportami, stammi accanto,

stringimi la mano finché ci sono
tendini e ossa, anche per te sia un dono
questa povera attesa dell'attesa.

I'll wish for myself then what I wish today
for these dear ones—a quiet, infinite
waiting for the quiet. Yet I admit
pride in still being alive keeps that at bay

among the living: I'm stripping it away
calmly from me, each day a little bit,
no more certain end, no less secret plot if it
has been inscribed, and who can say since when,

here on the very page on which I'm writing,
in the bible saved from pulp or flames. But you,
I beg meanwhile, bear with me, stay here, press

my hand in yours so tightly you caress
my tendons and my bones, and for you too
let it be a gift, this poor waiting for the waiting.

La casa di campagna dove leggere
George Eliot o E. M. Forster fino all'ora
della cenere e poi quando s'infervora
il silenzio delle siepi contendere

ori carte e primiera ai non ancora
scomparsi, è questa ormai l'unica immagine
che riesco a farmi della gioia in bilico
sulla frana del sonno. Ma la ignora

poco dopo, svegliandosi, la mente
infantilmente avida di luce
per rituffarsi impavida nell'orrida

dolcezza del presente: così incespica
un piede nell'altro, così si scuce
il rammendo invisibile del niente.

The house out in the country where I'd stay
awake reading Forster or George Eliot till
the hour of ashes and even then the still
of the hedges invigorating me to play

cards with those not yet gone away, I find
the image of those times the single thing
that brings me pleasure when I'm hovering
on the landslide of sleep. But then the mind,

awakening a little later, buoyed
by childish hunger for the light of day
to seize the horrid sweetness of the now

intrepidly, forgets it: and that's how
one foot trips over the other, that's the way
we undo the invisible mending of the void.

Andarsene, tornare, due pensieri
dolci fino alla morte in tre parole
sole, FERROVIE NORD MILANO, ieri
limpidamente stampate nel sole

del mattino, ora oscillanti sui poveri
trampoli del ricordo. Non ci vuole
molto per capire che i passeggeri
sanno poco o niente di ciò che duole

nella nostra memoria, che per loro
Auschwitz è un nome come tanti, un suono
senza storia. Li sento, più leggeri

dell'aria, sfiorarmi, fendere il buono
dell'aria, oh non esuli, frontalieri
dell'aria in viaggio fra la nebbia e l'oro.

To go away, to come back home again,
two notions sweet until I die in three
words only, RAILWAYS NORTH MILAN, back then
in the morning sun imprinted limpidly

and these days wobbling by upon the poor
stilts of remembrance. It's not hard to see
that all these passengers know little or
nothing of things that ache in our memory,

that Auschwitz is a name to them, just one
like any other, a sound that doesn't hold
any history. I feel them, lighter than

the air, as they graze me, split the goodness of
the air, not exiles, border commuters of
the air in transit between fog and gold.

Stanze per la musica di Adriano Guarnieri

Quare tristis — perché
sempre, nella veglia e nel sonno,
nell'omissione e nell'adempimento,
l'anima ci fa così male?
Noi che la custodiamo
senza amarla, senza conoscerla
nella gabbietta delle nostre ossa
come il vetro d'una lanterna
custodisce la fiamma
sappiamo soltanto che è lei,
lei che non ha né tendini né sangue,
la compagnia più sanguinosa.
Tu come lei invisibile
proteggici dal suo silenzio,
fa' che sentiamo in tempo la sua voce.

Così a volte succede che nel buio
si insanguini un volto, una mano
ci implori — così c'è
chi ignora e chi invece ha nel cuore
la comunione dei vivi e dei morti.

All'altro che siamo e non siamo,
alla nostra carcassa
che l'acqua piovana dilava,
che sotto il sole si fa secca e nera,
che i becchi dei corvi dilaniano
e il vento fa oscillare

Stanzas for the Music of Adriano Guarnieri

Quare tristis—why is it
always, when we wake and when we sleep,
in the omission and in the fulfillment,
that the soul is in such pain?
We who preserve her there
without loving her, without even knowing her
inside the little cage of our skeleton
the way the lantern glass
preserves the flame,
we only know that it is she,
she who has no tendons and no blood,
the bloodiest of all companions.
You, invisible like her,
protect us from her silence,
make it so we may hear her voice in time.

Thus in the darkness now and then a face
is stained with blood, a hand beseeches us—
thus there is someone who
disregards or else one who has in his heart
the communion of the living and the dead.

To the other that we are and we are not,
to our carcass
that the rainwater washes clean,
that dries up and turns black out in the sun,
that ravens pick to pieces with their beaks
and that flutters in the wind

così che pace mai non ha
sia grata e benedetta
l'oblazione di questo sangue
ut nobis Corpus et Sanguis fiat.

Sì — ma memento anche dei semivivi
e dei semimorti, di quanti
si dissanguano invano,
della ferita che non muta
in qualcosa di ricco e strano.

Ora sia più leggera la ferita,
d'un sangue più chiaro risplenda
sul cinereo la benda
occidua a chi affranto s'aduna
nei loculi accesi per l'infinita
conta dei tormenti o s'incruna
in bunker e cunicoli
per più lontane penitenze
sotto tegole rotte e fronde riarse
dal moto perpetuo degli acidi
— non folla, non esercito
ma persona una e triturata,
una e dispersa . . . A loro nell'orrendo
crepuscolo, nel vaneggiare
dell'aurora sia pace.

so that it never is at peace
let the oblation of this blood
be pleasing and consecrated
ut nobis Corpus et Sanguis fiat.

Yes—but a memento too of the half alive
and the half dead, of all those
who are bleeding now in vain,
of the wound that does not change
into something rich and strange.

Now let the wound be lighter, let it be
that the waning bandage shines with clearer blood
upon the ash-gray head
of an exhausted one who is gathered to
the burning tombs for an eternity
of countless torments or is threading through
bunkers and tunnels to
more distant penances
under the broken tiles and branches parched
by the perpetual motion of the acids
—not a crowd, not a multitude
but one person, one and scattered,
one and crushed to dust . . . To those in the horrid
twilight, those in the delirium
of dawn let there be peace.

Con raccapriccio, come ogni anno, spio
i passi falsi della primavera,
il suo esporsi scriteriato all'altera
scomunica del gelo e so che anch'io

ne ho colpa, che è anche per la mia impazienza
di vecchio che lei si butta così
allo sbaraglio. Mai che smetta di
sperare, fiorire a vanvera, senza

nient'altro nella mente oltre la cieca,
luminosa dolcezza del futuro . . .
Quale? Già, questo è l'insolente, oscuro
busillis, è lì che s'infila e spreca

l'ardore. Ma di che giubilo crepita
intanto, quanta gloria in tanta perdita.

In fear, as in every year, I watch the early
false steps of spring as she wanders everywhere,
exposing herself so madly to the surly
excommunication of ice and I have a share

of the blame for this, I can see, because an old
man's impatience is part of the reason she
rushes into the fray. Never does she hold
back in her hoping, flowering randomly

with nothing in mind but the blind and radiant
sweetness of the future . . . But which one?
Now here's the snag, so dark and insolent,
here's where her ardor sinks and comes undone.

Meanwhile, it crackles with a glorious
rejoicing, so much splendor in such loss.

Mio male, mio bene, così vicini
ormai che tante volte vi confondo,
che risse facevate quando il mondo
era pieno di luce e i teatrini

del cuore non scritturavano ombre
ma angeli e demoni in carne e ossa
e da tutte le parti, nella fossa
di chi rammenta, nelle quinte ingombre

di macerie, nei cessi, nel foyer
annerito dagli incendi ferveva
l'incauta vita . . . Certo, si solleva
ancora il sipario, ogni sera c'è

spettacolo — ma senza vincitori
né vinti, senza sangue, senza fiori.

My bad, my good, by now so close that I
confuse you often, how you used to fight
each other when the world was filled with light
and little theaters of the heart didn't hire

shadows for their roles but filled each one
with angels and demons in the flesh, on all
sides, in the pit of him who can recall,
in the toilets, in the wings that were overrun

with wreckage, in the foyer that was so
flame-blackened, life was reckless and it blazed . . .
Yes, it is true the curtain is still raised,
and every evening there is still a show—

but now there are no winners in the plays,
no losers, and no blood, and no bouquets.

Quanti fossero i pioppi che importanza
può avere? so che c'erano, che adesso
non ci sono, che a volte m'è concesso
di vederli, immenso fruscio, sostanza

visibile del vento — e so che è ancora
questa la linea che separa da
catastrofi nere o abbaglianti la
grigia dolcezza del giardino. Sfioralo

con gli occhi, soltanto, il sipario, lascia
che di là vada come sai che è andata,
che bruci la fabbrica bombardata
dalle fortezze volanti, che l'ascia

s'abbatta sulle betulle, che i morti
assassinino e perdonino i morti.

The poplars—what possible significance
in how many of them there were? I know that then
they were there, that now they're not, that now and again
it's given to me to see them, the immense

rustling, wind's visible substance—and I know
that this is still the line that keeps away
brilliant or black catastrophes from the gray
sweetness in the garden. Let just your eyes go

lightly over the curtain, let it all
go on the other side as you know it has,
let the factory the flying fortresses
bombarded burn to the ground, let axes fall

down on the clump of birch trees, let the dead
murder and give forgiveness to the dead.

Ci sono stato, non so quando (o è stato
un altro, e io ero l'altro): la vetrata
luminosa, tranquilla, colorata
appena, grigio su rosa, dal lato

d'un eterno crepuscolo . . . e al di là
d'un paravento o d'una tenda i flebili
cinguettii, i fiochi stridi di invisibili
rianimandi . . . È un miracolo se va

fino al turno di guardia della sera,
se ce la fa a raggiungere lo spigolo
più lontano del comodino il calcolo
del respiro. E in compenso come è vera

e vasta la gioia, come consente
lieta la mente al parlottio del niente.

I was here, I don't know when (or else it was
another, and I was the other): the window so
pale-tinted that its colors hardly show,
gray over rose, serene and luminous

beside an eternal twilight . . . and then past
a screen or curtain, plaintive chatter, all
the feeble cries of the invisible
revived . . . It's a miracle if it can last

until the evening shift comes on again,
if breath is measured out so it enables
making it all the way to the bedside table's
far corner. And in compensation, then,

how vast and real joy is, with what elation
the mind consents to idle conversation.

Camminerai sull'acqua per tornare
dove sei sempre stato. Intanto vivi
pagando vecchi debiti, coltivi
la tua puntigliosità militare,

accumuli prove a discolpa come
se la gioia che t'aspetta dovessi
davvero meritartela o potessi
perderla ancora, ostaggio d'un cognome

inventato da chissà quale mente
boriosa se lo si legge in Giovanni
20, 16. Quanti e che duri anni
a sentirti padre infinitamente

volendo essere figlio, a scongiurare
ferite, tu che le hai così care . . .

You'll walk on water so that you can go
back where you've always been. But while you wait
you live, you pay old debts, you cultivate
your military-style punctilio,

accumulating proof you're not to blame
as if you had to earn the joy that will
be yours in days to come or if you still
could lose it once more, hostage of a last name

born of a boastful brain, as we can see
in Saint John, chapter 20, verse 16.
How many and how hard the years have been,
feeling yourself a father endlessly

wishing to be a son, and trying to
ward off wounds, though they are so dear to you . . .

L'autunno ha a volte luci così terse
e, sugli alberi, rossi di così
atroce dolcezza che il cuore si
spezzerebbe vedendoli. In diverse

più innocue incombenze dunque si finge
assorbito e lascia che siano gli occhi
a incantarsene, a impregnarsene, sciocchi
e intrepidi come sono . . . Poi stinge

a poco a poco o forse trascolora
come fa, salendo, la luna, quel
tetro fulgore, scrudelisce nel
pulviscolo del tempo, e solo allora

uno ha il coraggio di dire quant'era
bello — più bello della primavera.

At times in autumn there are lights so clear
and, on the trees, reds of such terribly
ferocious sweetness that your heart would be
shattered to see them. So it will appear

preoccupied by a variety
of more innocuous tasks, but still permit
your eyes to charm and warm themselves in it,
brave and foolish as they are . . . And then you see

it fading bit by bit, but then again
perhaps it's changing color, as the moon
rising in its somber splendor soon
uncruels itself in time's dust. Only then

do you dare to say how beautiful a thing
it really was—more beautiful than spring.

Da qualche parte, Bosnia o Medioriente,
trafficano in morti, scambiano salme
con salme e persino, come se niente
fosse, con dei vivi. Vorrei scordarmene

e non riesco. Chi lo fisserà,
mi domando, il listino? quanti corpi
illacrimati per la libertà
d'un pilota? e i mutilati, gli storpi,

i ciechi a quanto stanno d'un intero?
Scherzo — no, imbroglio. Tento di nascondermi
qualcosa che non so, forse il più vero
dei desideri, essere loro, accludermi

allo zero che moltiplica, al niente
che è, al mai che fa aggio sul presente.

In places, the Middle East or Bosnia,
they trade the dead, exchanging one cadaver
for another one and even, as if it were
nothing, for some that are still alive. I'd rather

forget it, and I can't. Who will compile it,
the price list? I ask myself, how many unmourned
corpses to win the freedom of a pilot?
and the maimed ones and the crippled and the blind,

how much would they be worth in the entire
assessment? I'm joking—no, cheating. I try to hide
from something I don't know, the truest desire
perhaps, to be them, to close myself inside

the zero that multiplies, in the nothing that is, in
the never that holds a premium on the present.

Ci sono sere che vorrei guardare
da tutte la finestre delle strade
per cui passo, essere tutte le rade
ombre che vedo o immagino vegliare

nei loro fiochi santuari. Abbiamo,
sussurro passando, lo stesso sogno,
cancellare fino a domani il sogno
opaco, cruento del giorno, li amo

anch'io i vostri muri pallidamente
fioriti, i vostri sonnolenti acquari
televisivi dove i lampadari
nuotano come polpi, non c'è niente

che mi escluda tranne la serratura
chiusa che esclude voi dalla paura.

There are evenings when I wish I could look out
all the windows on the streets I pass through, be
all the occasional shadows that I see
or imagine who are still up and about

in their dim-lit sanctuaries. On the way
I murmur to myself, we share a dream,
to annul until tomorrow comes the dream,
fearful and unfathomable, of day,

I love them too, your pale walls patterned by
flowers, the floating chandeliers that pass
across the somnolent aquarium glass
of your television screens like octopi,

and there is nothing that keeps me out here
but the fastened locks that keep you from your fear.

Non sono poi così incerti i confine
del mondo: via Vitruvio, via Pisani,
via Bixio e, confusamente, i giardini
di via Palestro. Fuori è già domani:

aria di parate, di bombe al fosforo,
di cadaveri appesi a testa in giù.
Là si vivrà, forse, e anche con decoro
e, chissà, con qualche gloria — ma è più

facile non farcela, è più probabile
che l'asfalto ci inghiotta, che una statua
ci rovini sulla testa. Un'orribile
lebbra è già al lavoro, sbrana la fatua,

la luccicante . . . Ah stiamo qui, viviamo,
papà, mamma! dove vivi vi amo.

Then the world's borders aren't so dubious:
Pisani, Vitruvio, Bixio streets, and
in a rather confused way, Palestro's
gardens. Tomorrow's already out beyond:

an air of parades, of phosphorescent bombs,
cadavers hung up upside down. And that
is where we're going to live, perhaps, with some
decorum, and who knows, with some glory—but

it's easier not to manage, more probable
that asphalt's going to swallow us, that a statue is
going to fall on our heads. Already a horrible
leprosy's at work, it's devouring the fatuous,

the glittering . . . Ah, let's stay here, let's survive,
papa, mamma! where I love you alive.

Ospite, io, loro, o loro miei
nel giardino incantato da un crepuscolo
di fine estate? Non lo so, vorrei
tanto saperlo — sùbito, in articulo

vitae — e invece so solo che più niente
ci mancherà, che nessuna ferita
potrà più suppurare, che il presente
prima o poi ce la farà, avrà partita

vinta . . . Ma adesso basta. Chi si sogna
vivo coi suoi morti forse non è
vivo che lì, nel sogno, e non bisogna
svegliarlo — non ancora, non finché

fuori, nella luce, c'è quella macina
che stride, quella lamiera che abbacina.

I, their guest, or they mine in the enchanted
garden in the end-of-summer glow
of twilight? I don't know, but how I've wanted
to know—and quickly, *in articulo*

vitae—yet I know only that there isn't
a thing that will be missed, no wound will be
able to fester anymore, that the present
will make it sooner or later, it will see

victory . . . But enough for now. Whoever
lives, when he dreams, with all those dead of his
lives only in the dream, perhaps, and never
need be awakened—not yet, not till there is

outside in the light of day the sight of blinding
sheet metal and the creak of millstones grinding.

Mi sono distratto — oh, per poco, appena
quaranta, cinquant'anni — e mi ritrovo
di colpo, gli occhi abbarbagliati, in piena
vecchiaia, mia e del mondo. Niente è nuovo,

ora che le vivo, più delle cose
che ho vissuto aspettandole, aspettando
la vita, più delle, ma sì! famose
rose che ho colto come in trance, macchiandomi,

spesso e volentieri, di sangue . . . Eppure
c'ero anch'io quella volta, era il mio cuore,
erano i miei nervi, le mie giunture
a tremare di gioia e di terrore

per la tua venuta, sono sicuro
d'esserci stato — o era già il futuro?

I was distracted—a short while, it must be
only forty, fifty years—and, with my two
eyes bedazzled, I find myself suddenly
in old age, mine and the world's. Nothing is new,

now that I live them, more than the things I have
lived while I waited for them, and waited for life,
more than, oh yes, those famous roses that I've
gathered, ever so happily staining myself

over and over with blood, plucking them as
if I were in a trance . . . And yet it was I
who was there that time, it was my heart, it was
my nerves, my joints that trembled then with joy

and dread at your coming, I'm sure, I must have been
there—or was it already the future then?

Non so, non so ancora, direi un quartiere
fuori porta con vecchi capannoni
dismessi, un gasometro, ciminiere
senza fumo — sì, un quadro di Sironi

del '20–25 ma guastato,
corrotto dal tempo come il ritratto
di Dorian Gray. A far cosa? Be', da un lato
a vivere, forse — ma soprattutto

a sparire: un giorno o l'altro bisogna
pur cominciare e dove se non dove
anche l'alba e il tramonto hanno vergogna
del loro sangue e le volte che piove

sembra che piova ruggine, tritume
d'ossa, bambagia, celluloide, allume . . .

I don't know, no, I don't know yet, I'd guess
a place outside the city, a gas tank, some
smokeless smokestacks, empty warehouses—
yes, a painting of Sironi's from

'20 or '25, but moldering
with time's corruptions like the picture of
Dorian Gray. To do what? For one thing,
to live, perhaps—but to disappear, above

all else: it's something I must start to do
one day or another, and where if not where
the dawn's ashamed of its blood, the sunset too,
and those times when it rains it seems the air

is full of rust and celluloid, is full
of alum, bits of bone, and cottonwool.

Dopo la vita cosa? ma altra vita,
si capisce, insperata, fioca, uguale,
tremito che non s'arresta, ferita
che non si chiude eppure non fa male

— non più, non tanto. Lentamente come
risucchiati all'indietro da un'immensa
moviola ogni cosa riavrà il suo nome,
ogni cibo apparirà sulla mensa

dov'era, sbiadito, senza profumo . . .
Bella scoperta. È un pezzo che la mente
sa che dove c'è arrosto non c'è fumo
e viceversa, che fra tutto e niente

c'è un pietoso armistizio. Solo il cuore
resiste, s'ostina, povero untore.

After this life? another one, so we
understand, unhoped for, faint, unvarying;
unending tremor, a wound eternally
open (and yet we never feel a thing)

—no more, and not so much. As though they'd been
sucked slowly backward by a huge moviola
every thing will possess its name again
and on the table, faded, with no aroma,

every meal will reappear . . . What a surprise.
For a long time the mind has been aware
that where there's smoke there isn't fire and vice
versa, and that all and nothing share

a pitiful armistice. Only the stubborn heart,
the poor plague-spreader, resists and stands apart.

Svegliami, ti prego, succede ancora
d'implorare in un sogno a questa tenera
età, aiutami, fa' che non sia vera
l'oscena materia del buio. Sfiora

allora davvero una mano il mio
corpo assiderato e di colpo so
d'averti chiamata e che non saprò
più niente.

Wake me, I beg you, it's still going on,
pleading at this tender age in a dream,
help me, and make it so that the obscene
stuff of the darkness isn't real. And then

I really feel a hand upon me brushing
my frozen body and suddenly I know
that I've called out to you and that I'll know
nothing more.

Nell'ora, ormai, della cenere
a pochi passi il corso brulicava
di commerci frenetici e ingannevoli
e di delitti consumati in sogno
quando per contagio di quel che resta
d'un antico ricetto di sventure,
cinque camini e sei finestre in tutto
di mattoni color sangue, avviliti
ora, loro, da miasmi micidiali
più dell'intero un tempo dal famoso
flagello di cui si legge nei libri
considerai con l'immaginazione
l'immensa prateria purgatoriale
che da quella fronte invisibilmente
sin quasi agli invisibili bastioni
aveva per suo centro San Carlino
come l'ostia la sua goccia di sangue
quando inginocchiato premevo gli occhi
con le mani per vera contrizione
dopo un fantasticato sacrilegio
e pensai che lui, sì, non gli spagnoli
ci aveva ammassati lì come agnelli
per sterminarci. Che colpe, le stesse
o altre m'inchiodano bolgia a bolgia
a questo rione dove tante volte
sono nato e morto e resuscitato
da perderne il conto, tiepida, tetra
giungla battuta palmo a palmo in cerca
di vaghe assoluzioni — così andavo
domandando al mio cuore e rivedevo
intanto di seguito alle reliquie
della strage, sul medesimo lato
di quella fenditura di mannaia

In the time, now, of ashes, just a few
steps away the avenue was swarming
with trades that were chaotic and deceitful
and crimes that were committed in a dream
when, owing to the contamination of
what's still left of that refuge of misfortunes,
five chimneys and six window frames in all,
constructed of blood-colored bricks that are
humiliated now by murderous
miasmas more than the whole of it once was
by the famous plague we read about in books,
in my imagination I considered
the enormous purgatorial prairie
that facing from that side invisibly
almost as far as the invisible ramparts
had San Carlino's church as centerpiece
just as the host had had its drop of blood
when down upon my knees I pressed my hands
against my eyes to make a true contrition
after I'd fantasized a sacrilege,
thinking that it was he and not the Spanish
who'd crowded us in there like little lambs
to slaughter us. Such sins as these, or others,
have nailed me bolgia after bolgia to
this neighborhood where I was born and died
and brought to life again so many times
that I've lost count of them, a tepid, dismal
jungle beaten inch by inch in search of
vague absolutions—so I carried on
inquiring of my heart and in the meantime,
following the relics of the disaster,
on the same side of the axe's cut where I
was crawling all around, I saw again

dove stavo strisciando, un altro luogo
d'abominio e salvezza, un cinemino
di puttane a poco prezzo da poco
redento in supermarket. Mai scambiata,
s'intende, una parola: se ci andavo
così spesso alle dieci, dieci e mezza
di mattina mentre a casa pensavano
che fossi al Parini o al Carducci era
per amore infinito di quel buio
pagato in anticipo in stropicciate
agonizzanti amlire, anestesia
o abiura dei miei grotteschi rimorsi
d'adolescente. E non potrei giurarlo
ma forse fu proprio lì, nell'arsura
atroce degli intervalli, aspettando
che quel buio tornasse come un balsamo
su un'ustione che cominciai a pregare
come faccio ancora, e sempre in latino,
ogni volta che per troppo silenzio
o troppa luce il cuore si contorce
ignominiosamente. Ma perché,
mi chiedo, già allora, se erano ancora
tutti vivi? e rispondo che l'angoscia
ha astuzie che la ragione non può
sventare — o forse era precisamente
per loro, perché niente succedesse,
perché nessuno avesse l'impudenza
di morire me vivo; e invece l'onta
della morte si sarebbe abbattuta
di schianto, subdolamente, nel giro
di pochissimi anni sul decoro
della famiglia . . . Incredibile: c'erano
altri sconvolgimenti, altre catastrofi
oltre quelli delle mie inadempienze!

another place of abomination and
salvation, a little movie theater
of low-priced whores redeemed not long ago
into a supermarket. Not one single
word, you understand, was ever exchanged:
if I went there so many times at ten,
ten-thirty in the morning while at home
they thought I was at Parini or Carducci,
it was out of limitless love of that darkness
that I had paid for in advance with crumpled
dying AM-lire, the anesthesia
or abjuration of an adolescent's
grotesque pangs of conscience. And although
I couldn't swear to it, perhaps it was
right there, in the ferocious scorching heat
of intermission, waiting for that darkness
to come back like a balm upon a burn
that I began to pray the way that I
still do, always in Latin, each time the heart
because of too much light or too much silence
writhes ignominiously. But why already
back then, I ask myself, if they were all
still living? and my answer is that anguish
has its own wiles that reason cannot thwart—
or was it precisely because of them, because
nothing had happened and no one had had
the impudence to die while I survived?
although it was the case that the offense
of death would be inflicted, suddenly
and underhandedly, in the course of just
a few short years, on the decorum of
the family . . . How incredible: there were
other upheavals, other catastrophes
other than those of my delinquincies!

Ma non anticipiamo, in quel momento
il problema ero ancora io, il mio
rannicchiarmi nel buio scricchiolante
del cinema Modena come un feto
dentro il ventre materno e come uscirne
senza strangolarmi. La relativa
normalità dei miei cinquanta e passa
anni successivi può comprovare
l'accaduto, non spiegarlo: se so
d'essermi liberato del terrore
non so ancora per quanto, né in che modo,
e credo che non meno inconsapevole
sia stato secoli fa, a qualche metro,
l'attonito sciamare dei superstiti
della peste verso le meraviglie
di un'usuale carestia. Di loro
niente, nei libri o altrove; né dei morti
portati via a carrettate, sepolti
come viene in qualche foppone, all'ombra
d'un filare di gelsi. Quanto all'ospite
del cinema-fantasma, al qui scrivente,
stia un po' zitto adesso, se n'ha abbastanza
delle sue querimonie: nessun nesso
fra il resistere a dispetto dei santi
di quelle sante macerie, quei ruderi
d'un'antica misericordia e
questo abietto monumento invisibile
alla sua infanzia interminata. Meglio
muoversi, affrettare l'incerto passo
prima che la cenere solidifichi
alla volta del gran fiume imminente
e lì svoltare, perdersi, svanire.

But not to get too far ahead, at that
moment the problem was still me, still my
nestling there inside the crackling darkness
of the Modena movie theater like a fetus
inside its mother's womb and how I could
come out of it without strangling. The relative
normality of my succeeding fifty
years and counting can confirm the case,
but not explain it: if I know myself
to have been liberated from the terror
I still don't know how far, or in what fashion,
and I believe that no less unaware
was the swarming in astonishment
centuries ago, just a stone's throw,
of plague survivors toward the marvels of
an ordinary famine. Nothing of them,
in books or anywhere else, nor of the dead
borne off by cartloads, buried as it happens
in some enormous mass grave, in the shade
of a row of mulberry trees. As for the guest
of the ghost-movie, who's writing here, it's time
for him to shut his mouth, no one could stand
any more of his bellyaching: no connection
between his resisting, in despite of all
the saints of those sainted ruins, those remains
of an ancient misericordia and this
tawdry invisible monument to his
unterminated childhood. Better to be
moving, quickening his uncertain pace,
before the ashes can solidify,
toward the flow of the great oncoming river,
to turn there, lose himself, and disappear.

da BARLUMI DI STORIA (2002)

from GLIMMERS OF HISTORY (2002)

Smettila, hai capito? di immaginarci.
Siamo dove siamo, non dove a te
piacerebbe che fossimo ogni sera
poco prima del niente
per non perderci d'occhio, per tenerci
oh amorevolmente! sotto controllo . . .
Fai tutto difficile, come sempre.
Hai sempre reso tutto più difficile.
Anche allora, defilarci lasciandoti
a una normalissima orfanità
è diventato un caso, una catastrofe,
un sopruso atroce, contro natura . . .
E adesso, con questa tua fissazione
di rimetterci in scena ogni momento,
tu regista, tu solo spettatore,
curando ogni dettaglio, quella luce
che da rosa si fa viola, quell'ombra
sempre più evanescente
che la sedia disegna sulla ghiaia,
quella mano d'adulto che si posa
in primissimo piano
su una mano più piccola e più bianca,
cosa ti riprometti? Non dirai
che è per noi che lo fai . . . Su, lascia perdere,
non volere dal tempo
quello che il tempo non potrà non darti:
prega per la nostra quiete, e basta.

Stop conjuring us up, do you understand?
We are right where we are, and not where you
would like to have us every single evening
just before the nothingness
so that you don't lose sight of us, so that
you keep us—oh, so lovingly!—under control . . .
You're making everything difficult, as always.
You've always made everything more difficult.
Back then, our cutting out and leaving you
to an extremely normal orphanhood
became a disaster, a catastrophe,
a hideous injustice, against nature . . .
And now, with this fixation that you have
to bring us back on camera every second,
with you the director, you the sole spectator,
seeing to every detail, to that light
changing from rose to violet, to that ever
more evanescent shadow
that the chair projects across the gravel,
that hand of an adult that comes to settle
in an extreme closeup
upon a whiter and much smaller hand,
what is it that you're hoping for? You can't
say that you're doing it for us . . . Come on,
just let it go, don't ask
of time what time can't fail to give you: pray
for our repose, and that's an end of it.

In questa gli assomiglia
ancora di più, guarda: gli stessi occhi
leggermente obliqui, il sinistro
appena un po' più grande
dell'altro, e quell'accenno di sorriso
ferocemente mite. Sullo sfondo,
dietro file di capanni sfuocati,
l'invisibile, sconfinata
mutezza del mare. Matura
anche in questo silenzio, in questo minimo
surrogato d'eternità
il tempo dei falsari e dei carnefici.

In this one he looks even more
like him; here, take a look: he has the same
eyes, slightly slanting, with the left one just
the tiniest little bit
bigger than the other, and the same hint
of a fiercely tender smile. And in the background
behind the rows of out-of-focus huts,
the boundless, invisible
muteness of the sea. It ripens
even in this silence, in this slightest
surrogate of eternity
the time of forgers and executioners.

Mai davvero felice e mai del tutto
infelice — oh, l'ho capito; e mi regolo.
Ma pensare la gioia, almeno quello:
pensarla! e qualche volta, senza farsi
troppe idee, senza montarsi la testa,
annusarla, sfiorarla con le dita
come se fosse (non lo è?) l'avanzo
della vita d'un santo, una reliquia . . .

O forse la felicità
è solo degli altri, d'un altro tempo,
d'un'altra vita e a noi non è possibile
che recitarla come viene viene,
a soggetto, ostinandoci a inseguire
la parte di noi stessi
in un vecchio, bizzarro canovaccio
senza capo né coda . . .

E per tutto il resto, per quello
che in tutto questo tempo
ho sprecato o frainteso, per l'amore
preso e non dato, avuto e non ridato
nella mia ingloriosa carriera
di marito, di padre e di fratello
ci sarà giustizia, là, un altro appello?
Niente più primavera,
mi viene da pensare, se allo sperpero
non ci fosse rimedio, se morire
fosse dolce soltanto per chi muore.

(1988–91)

Never really happy, never quite
unhappy—oh, I got it; and I act
accordingly. But to think of joy, at least
to think of it! and sometimes, without getting
too many ideas, without getting a big head,
to breathe a whiff of it, to run my fingers
over it as if it were (and isn't it?)
the remains of a saint's life, a holy relic . . .

Or maybe happiness is just
of other people, of another time,
of another life, and all that we can do
is play the part and take it as it comes,
improvising, persisting in pursuing
the role of ourselves
in an old and odd scenario that has
neither head nor tail . . .

And for all the rest, for what
through all this time
I've wasted or misunderstood, for love
taken and not given, had and not given back
in my inglorious career
as a husband, as a father and a brother
will there be justice, there, another
appeal? Never springtime here
again, it occurs to me, if there wouldn't be
a remedy for this squandering, if dying
were sweet only for the one who dies.

(1988–91)

I film porno mi annoiano.
Ma andare insieme in uno di quei cinema
dove si fa di tutto
tranne guardarli, dove tutti vagano
come anime in pena
tra fila e fila in cerca di qualcuno,
uomo o donna, pagante o a pagamento,
da portarsi nei cessi,
ah questo no che non mi annoierebbe!
Quante volte, mio puro e altero amore,
sei stata a tua insaputa nel girone,
quante volte mi sono mescolato
alla torma inquieta dei dannati
per spiare noi due coi loro occhi,
per vederci come loro s'inventano
che siamo, che ti tocco, che respiri . . .

(1993)

Pornographic movies bore me.
But going together to one of those theaters
where people do everything
but watch the movies, where the customers
like souls in torment go
from row to row all looking for someone,
man or woman, paying or to be paid,
to take into the bathrooms,
no, that is something that would never bore me!
How many times, my pure and haughty love,
you've been in the circle without knowing it,
how many times I've blended myself in
amid the restless multitude of the damned
to spy upon the two of us with their eyes,
to look at us the way that they imagine
how we are, how I touch you, how you breathe . . .

(1993)

Mai avuto, io, il doppio dei tuoi anni.
Ma cosa dico? certo che li ho avuti,
solo che tu non c'eri, eri, vediamo,
a Padova, o forse Venezia, intenta
a qualche tua storia d'irresistibile
ventiduenne — e in fondo cosa importa
in base a quale calcolo o magia
la ragazza che eri è diventata
l'incresciosamente giovane donna
che sarai finché vivo e io per non perderti
un malato che da vent'anni s'ingegna
di non morire? Non lasciarmi né ora
né prima, mi sembra a volte di dire
non so con che cuore, e a chi delle due.

There was never a time when I was twice your age.
What am I saying? Of course there was such a time,
only you weren't here, you were, let's see,
in Padua, maybe Venice, intent on some
of your history as an irresistible
twenty-two-year-old—and really in the end
what does it matter what charm or calculation
transformed the young girl that you were into
the regrettably young woman that you'll be
as long as I'm alive, a sick man who
to keep from losing you has pushed himself
for twenty years not to die. Don't leave me either
now or first, I sometimes seem to say,
but with which heart, and to which one of the two?

Infinitamente mi piacerebbe
suonare il pianoforte, e qualche volta
con poca modestia considero
che se in tempo di guerra
non avessi, causa i bombardamenti,
interrotto per sempre le lezioni
tanto volute da mia madre
a compenso o rivalsa, ora lo so,
d'un suo remoto sacrificio
a quest'ora, chissà . . . Ma poi mi dico
che è di un'altra delle sue passioni
che mi sono, come ho potuto,
fatto carico — e penso che a rifletterci
in ogni caso è proprio questo
da quando lei è morta
il modo in cui amo le cose
che amo di più, restandone alla larga,
avendone un po' di paura,
credendoci ma sempre di sfuggita
come credo all'esistenza di Dio.

It would please me enormously to be
able to play the piano, and there are times
when with scant modesty it seems to me
that if I hadn't
during the war, because of the bombardments,
permanently interrupted the lessons
my mother had so passionately desired
in revenge or compensation, I now know,
for a sacrifice that she'd made long ago,
today, who knows? . . . But then I tell myself
it's another of her passions
that, far as I've been able to, I've taken
upon myself—and I think, reflecting on it,
in any case it's really,
ever since she died,
the way I love the things
I love the most, keeping my distance from them,
being a bit afraid of them,
believing in them but always incidentally,
the way that I believe that God exists.

Cantano di paura nel giardino
sterposo, pieno di buio, gli storni
del convento. Nessuno più di lei
fortifica la voce,
neanche l'amore. Più tardi, già mattina,
un dolce servitore, per vecchiezza
stropicciando le sillabe, ci dice
che questo fanno gli storni: da ogni lato
d'ogni campo o giardino
che stimano loro dimora
mettono sentinelle perché stridano
se qualcuno, bestia o persona,
ne oltrepassa i confini . . . E che distinguono
fra un pericolo e l'altro,
fra spoliazione e morte . . . Così gridano
quel loro canto che sempre è di terrore
ma a volta a volta varia, ci sussurra
il nostro informatore. Ma di quanto
e come varia non sa dire, e neanche ha posto,
ci sembra, fra i suoi pensieri canuti.

(1988)

They're singing out of fear in the scrubby
garden full of darkness, the starlings
of the cloister. Nothing fortifies
their voices more than that,
not even love. Later, when it's morning,
a gentle servant, crumpling his syllables
out of old age, explains to us
that this is what starlings do: on every side
of every field or garden
they think of as their home
they post their sentinels so that they'll shriek
if anyone, man or beast,
crosses their boundaries . . . And that they distinguish
between different kinds of danger,
between pillaging and death . . . And so they screech
their song, which is always one of terror, though
from time to time it varies, our informant
whispers to us. But how and by how much
it varies he can't say, nor does it even have
a place, so it seems to us, in his hoary thoughts.

(1988)

Il rimorchiatore che passa
senza rumore (ha i doppi vetri
la mia stanza d'albergo)
mentre il sole obliquamente trionfa
su non so più che fiume — la pozzanghera
gelata che s'affolla
di pattinatori festanti
nella luce perlacea del crepuscolo —
a spese di chi, mi domando,
anzi di quanti, quale contrappeso
di umiliazioni e di dolori
sarà necessario per bilanciare
la perfezione di due istanti
alla corte dei conti dell'orrore?
Ma non c'è rimorso, vedo, che valga
a togliere splendore a quelle immagini.

The tugboat passing by
without a sound (my hotel room
has double-paned windows)
while the sun exults obliquely
over I don't know what river—the frozen
puddle where jubilant
skaters swarm
in the pearly light of dusk—
at whose expense, I ask myself,
or rather of how many, what counterweight
of sorrows and humiliations
will be required to balance
the perfection of two moments
at the court of audit of atrocities?
And yet, I see, there's no remorse that's worth
taking the splendor from those images.

Ci sono stati, nel '43,
anche due russi. Di uno, conducente
e forse, si diceva,
comproprietario sotto falso nome
d'una vecchia automobile a metano
noleggiata con cautele infinite
per un viaggio d'andata e non ritorno
dalle parti di Como o di Luino
e per spiritata magrezza identico,
l'ho capito più tardi, a Mischa Auer
ci si occupò per un paio di sere,
non di più: nella cerchia
degli ex villeggianti murati vivi
a aspettare il tam tam di radio Londra
fra la salita a fianco della chiesa
e il sentiero della torre romana
una vittoria dell'Armata rossa
faceva mille volte più notizia
dei piccoli misteri d'un borghese
sospettabilissimo, per età,
d'essere un disertore. Mentre l'altra,
la contessa di due ville più avanti,
al secolo dama di compagnia
o meglio (ma era meglio non saperlo)
cameriera della zia di mio padre,
ah, con lei era tutta un'altra cosa,
con lei ci si poteva sbizzarrire
all'infinito, balli a corte, fughe
in slitta sulla neve,
arresti, fucilazioni ma tutto
come in un album di fotografie
o nelle copertine di Beltrame,
nessuna ricaduta sul presente,

There were, in the year of 1943,
two Russians there as well. With one, a driver
and maybe, so people said,
also co-owner under a false name
of an old automobile that ran on methane
and that was rented out with infinite
precautions for a one-way journey to
the countryside near Como or Luino
and in his frenzied leanness the spitting image,
as I later realized, of Mischa Auer,
we were concerned for just a couple of evenings,
no more than that: in the circle
of the ex-vacationers walled up alive
waiting for the Radio London grapevine
between the slope beside the church
and the pathway of the Roman tower
one victory by the Red Army made
a thousand times more news than did the petty
mysteries of a civilian who was highly
open to suspicion, because of his age,
of being a deserter. While the other,
the countess who was living two villas away,
out in the world a lady in waiting or even
better (but it was better not to know)
and now the lady's maid of my father's aunt,
ah, with her it was quite another thing,
with her we could indulge our fancies to
the infinite, with balls at court and flights
in a sleigh across the snow,
arrests and executions by firing squad,
but all as if it were in a photo album
or else on magazine covers by Beltrame,
without any repercussions in the present,

neanche le congetture più cruente
sulla sua metamorfosi
da nobildonna zarista a domestica
avrebbero mai potuto incrinare
la cieca fiducia di noi sfollati
nel provvidenziale genio strategico
di Stalin così come, d'altro lato,
le bombe che ci piovevano in testa
non ostacolavano il nostro slancio
verso i liberatori americani.
Quanto a lei, non parlava. Camminando
strascinava i piedi dentro pantofole
di panno due o tre misure più grandi
non senza una qualche solennità
e muoveva di continuo le labbra
in un silenzio vagamente ostile.
Anni imprecisabili, in ogni caso
portati molto male. Si chiamava
Nadia. E il patronimico? Mai saputo,
adesso che ci penso, il patronimico.

not even the bloodiest of our speculations
about her metamorphosis from Czarist
noblewoman into a domestic
would ever have been capable of making
a crack in the blind faith we evacuees
had in the providential strategic genius
of Stalin, just as, on the other hand,
the bombs that they rained down upon our heads
didn't obstruct our enthusiasm for
the Americans who liberated us.
As for her, she didn't talk. And when she walked
she dragged her feet along the ground in cloth
slippers two or three sizes too large for her
though not without a certain solemnity
and as she walked along she moved her lips
continually in a vaguely hostile silence.
Indeterminable years, in any case
borne very badly. Her name was Nadia.
Her patronymic? We never knew what it was,
now that I think of it, her patronymic.

L'hanno picchiato a sangue, non a morte
il figlio mezzo scimunito
della fiorista del paese
che girava fischiando « Giovinezza »
due, al massimo tre giorni
prima del 25 aprile.
Era fascista? Certo — come quelli
che l'hanno preso a pugni
erano uno di Masnago, gli altri
di Induno: per esserci nati.
Mai più saremmo stati, lì da noi,
così atrocemente innocenti.

They beat him bloody, although not to death,
the halfwit son of the woman
who owned the local flower shop,
who went around whistling "Giovinezza"
two, no more than three
days before the twenty-fifth of April.
Was he a Fascist? Sure, he was—the way
that those who pounded him
were one of them from Masnago and the rest
from Induno: by being born there.
Never would we, there in our place, be so
hideously innocent again.

Le luci di Milano — poca cosa,
lo so, in quel primissimo dopoguerra
con più macerie che case, più scheletri
che armadi per nasconderli,
ma sfolgoranti e come ai fievoli occhi
del ragazzo fattosi di campagna
in tre anni d'esilio, quando il viale
che portava al cancello
scompariva crudelmente ogni sera
nell'osceno incantesimo del buio
e ai tanti pollicini della terra
il fiato bastava sì e no a sperare
che alla fine dell'infausta trasferta
nel labirinto dell'anestesia
le cose sarebbero state ancora
lì ad aspettarli. Ah niente più paura,
adesso! la città restava sveglia
per tutti, la città non scompariva
mai! proprio come avevo immaginato
di Parigi, di Londra, di New York
sugli amati romanzi . . . Cominciava
così, prendendo (quasi alla lettera)
lucciole per lanterne,
da capo o per sempre la vita.

The lights of Milan—a little thing, I know,
back then, right after the war ended, with
more rubble than houses, and more skeletons
than closets to hide them in,
but radiant and how to a boy's eyes
that had been weakened in the countryside
through three years of exile, when the lane
that led down to the gate
would cruelly disappear in the obscene
enchantment of the darkness every evening
and for so many Tom Thumbs of the earth
breathing more or less sufficed for hoping
that at the end of the unhappy transfer
into the labyrinth of anesthesia
things would still be the way they were before
and waiting there for them. Ah, no more fear,
not now! because the city stayed awake
for everyone, it didn't disappear,
not ever! it was just the way I had
imagined Paris, London, and New York
in the novels that I loved . . . And so it was
that, taking (almost literally)
lightning bugs for lanterns,
life started from the top again, for good.

Ricordo troppe cose dell'Italia.
Ricordo Pasolini
quando parlava di quant'era bella
ai tempi del fascismo.
Cercavo di capirlo, e qualche volta
(impazzava, ricordo,
il devastante ballo del miracolo)
mi è sembrato persino di riuscirci.
In fondo, io che ero più giovane
d'una decina d'anni,
avrei provato qualcosa di simile
tornando dopo anni
sui devastati luoghi del delitto
per la Spagna del '51, forse
per la Russia di Brežnev . . .
Ma ricordo anche lo sgomento,
l'amarezza, il disgusto
nella voce di Paolo Volponi
appena si seppero i risultati
delle elezioni del '94.
Era molto malato,
sapeva di averne ancora per poco
e di lì a poco, infatti, se n'è andato.
Di Paolo sono stato molto amico,
di Pasolini molto meno,
ma il punto non è questo. Il punto
è che è tanto più facile
immaginare d'essere felici
all'ombra d'un potere ripugnante
che pensare di doverci morire.

I remember too many things about Italy.
I remember Pasolini
when he talked about how beautiful it was
in the days of Fascism.
I tried to understand him, and sometimes
(I remember the devastating
dance of the miracle was running wild)
it seemed to me that I had managed it.
After all, I, who was younger than he was
by a good ten years,
would have felt something similar
going back after years
over those devastated scenes of crime
for the Spain of 1951, perhaps
for the Russia of Brezhnev . . .
But I remember also the dismay,
the bitterness, the disgust
in Paolo Volponi's voice
as soon as the results of the election
of 1994 had become known.
He was very sick,
he knew he only had a short time left
and, in fact, a short time later he was gone.
Paolo and I had always been close friends,
Pasolini and I were much less so.
But that is not the point. The point
is that it's so much easier
to imagine being happy
in the shadow of a repugnant power
than it is to think we have to die in it.

Si farà una gran fatica, qualcuno
direbbe che si muore — ma a quel punto
ogni cosa che poteva succedere
sarà successa e noi
davanti agli occhi non avremo
che la calma distesa del passato
da ripassare senza fretta
fermando ogni tanto l'immagine,
tornando un po' indietro, ogni tanto,
per capire meglio qualcosa,
per assaporare un volto, un vestito . . .
Sì, tutto in bianco e nero, se Dio vuole.
E tutto, anche le foglie che crescono,
anche i figli che nascono,
tutto, finalmente, senza futuro.

It's going to be a great effort, somebody
might say we're going to die—but at that point
everything that could have happened
will have happened and we
will have nothing before our eyes
but the calm expanse of the past
to be passed through again without haste,
freezing an image every now and then,
backing it up a little, now and then,
to understand something better,
to savor a face, a dress . . . Yes, everything
in black and white, if God should will it so.
And everything, even the growing leaves,
even the children being born,
everything, finally, without a future.

da SULL'ACQUA (2003)

from ON WATER (2003)

Sull'acqua

Scolpite nella pietra o impresse a fuoco
su pareti d'acciaio,
tracciate con il minio o con il sangue,
tatuate sulla pelle o nel cuore

lettera dopo lettera
sillaba dopo sillaba
le parole sbiadiscono, svaniscono,
perdono senso e suono

secolo dopo secolo
ritornano tutte a ritroso
a inesistere insieme

dov'erano in principio, nella mente
di chi non scrive — tutte tranne quelle
scritte sull'acqua

On Water

Carved into stone or incised with flame
on walls of steel,
traced with red lead or outlined in blood,
tattooed on the skin or in the heart,

letter after letter
syllable after syllable
the words fade, they vanish, evanesce,
they lose sound and sense

century after century
they all return in reverse
to inexist together

where they were in the beginning, in the mind
of one who does not write—all except those
written on water

da ULTIMI VERSI (2006)

from LAST POEMS (2006)

Canzone della nuova era

Bisognerà riabituarsi
a contarli per numeri romani
(di sicuro qualcuno
si ricorda ancora come si fa)
gli anni che son passati
e quelli ahinoi che passeranno
in questa nuova era
della nostra tragicomica storia.
Il problema è da dove, esattamente,
far partire il conteggio:
dalla discesa in campo
o dall'ascesa al trono,
dalla prima vittoria elettorale
o dall'ultima, quella
che ha segnato di sé il nuovo millennio?
O sarà invece il caso
d'andare più indietro, molto più indietro,
per esempio all'ingresso nella loggia
o a quando la coscienza del paese
ha cominciato a modellarsi
sui palinsesti di canale cinque?
Sarebbe già più d'un ventennio, allora,
più d'un ventennio . . .

Song of the New Era

We'll need to rehabituate ourselves
to counting them in Roman numerals
(surely there must be
someone who still remembers how to do it),
the years already passed
and those that, alas for us, have yet to pass
in this new era
of our tragicomic history.
The difficulty is from where, exactly,
to start the count:
from the descent into the field
or the ascent to the throne,
from the first electoral victory
or the last, the one
that in itself marked the new millennium?
Or will it be the case
that we need to go further back, much further back,
for instance the admission to the lodge
or else to when the country's consciousness
began to be shaped
by the schedule of shows on Channel 5?
Then that would be more than twenty years already,
more than twenty years . . .

Canzone del danno e della beffa

Stillicidio di delitti, terribile:
si distruggono vite,
si distruggono posti di lavoro,
si distrugge la giustizia, il decoro
della convivenza civile.
E intanto l'imprenditore del nulla,
il venditore d'aria fritta,
forte coi miserabili
delle sue inindagabili ricchezze,
sorride a tutto schermo
negando ogni evidenza, promettendo
il già invano promesso e l'impossibile,
spacciando per paterno
il suo osceno frasario da piazzista.
Mai così in basso, così simile
(non solo dirlo, anche pensarlo duole)
alle odiose caricature
che da sempre ci infangano e sfigurano . . .
Anche altrove, lo so,
si santifica il crimine, anche altrove
si celebrano i riti
del privilegio e dell'impunità
trasformati in dottrina dello stato.
Ma solo a noi, già fradici
di antiche colpe e remissioni,
a noi prima untori e poi vittime
della peste del secolo
è toccata, con il danno, la beffa,
una farsa in aggiunta alla sventura.

Song of Insult and of Injury

How terrible, the steady drip of crimes:
destroying lives,
destroying jobs,
destroying justice and the dignity
of civil society.
And all the while the entrepreneur of nothing,
the peddler of hot air,
powerful with the miserable
because of his wealth beyond investigation,
smiles in widescreen
denying all the evidence, promising
already empty impossible promises,
passing off as paternal
the smutty patter of a traveling salesman.
Never so low before, so like
(it hurts not just to say it, even to think it)
those odious caricatures
that have always dirtied and disfigured us . . .
In other places, I know,
they sanctify crime, in other places too
they solemnize the rites
of privilege and impunity
transformed into the doctrine of the state.
But only among us, already rotten
with ancient guilts and remissions, only with us
who first were spreaders and then victims of
the plague of the century
is insult added to the injury,
a farce that's folded in with the misfortune.

Tempus tacendi

Nessuno, credo, potrebbe seriamente mettere in dubbio l'importanza — l'importanza decisiva rispetto all'intero — delle ultime pagine di un romanzo, delle ultime battute di una sinfonia, degli ultimi minuti di una partita di calcio.

Termpus tacendi . . . Una fitta quasi insostenibile di felicità al pensiero che un giorno o l'altro potrei davvero leggere Dickens e Tolstoj, andare al cinema di pomeriggio, ascoltare i quartetti di Beethoven e i lieder di Schubert senza doverne rendere conto a nessuno.

Pensare all'anima — non per salvarla: per goderne.

È impossibile guardare il tempo senza vedere la morte, così come è impossibile guardare il mare aperto senza vedere l'orizzonte. Uno, per non vederla, dovrebbe passare tutta la vita di profilo come l'*one-eyed jack*, il povero fante monocolo delle carte da gioco. E il bello è che anche la morte, come l'orizzonte, è sempre alla stessa distanza.

7.9.91. Nei giornali di oggi, servizi sulla scoperta del gene della longevità da parte di un gruppo di scienziati americani. Sembra che uomini e donne potranno un giorno disporre di una vita lunghissima, ultrasecolare. Mi sembra legittimo chiedersi (ma negli articoli che ho letto nessuno se lo chiede): per farne che cosa?

No one, I believe, could seriously doubt the importance—the decisive importance with respect to the whole—of the final pages of a novel, the final notes of a symphony, the final minutes of a soccer match.

Tempus tacendi . . . A nearly unendurable pang of happiness at the thought that one day or another I might actually be able to read Dickens and Tolstoy, go to the movies in the afternoon, listen to Beethoven's quartets and Schubert's lieder without having to give an account of them to anyone.

To consider the soul—not to save it: to savor it.

It's impossible to look at time without seeing death, just as it's impossible to look at the open sea without seeing the horizon. To not see it, one would have to spend his whole life looking sideways like the poor one-eyed jack in a deck of playing cards. And the beauty of it is that even death, like the horizon, is always at the same distance.

9/7/91. In today's newspapers, stories about the discovery of the gene for longevity by a group of American scientists. It seems that men and women will one day have an extremely long lifespan at their disposal, more than a hundred years. It seems to me legitimate to wonder (but no one wonders about it in the articles that I read): to do what with it?

Ho sempre pensato che l'ultimità (so che questa parola non esiste, ma per il momento non sono disposto a rinunciarvi o sostituirla) sia la più preziosa, la più inebriante delle dolcezze. Ma come calcolarla senza spavento? Un condannato a morte potrebbe essere per una notte il più felice degli uomini se la felicità non gli fosse nascosta o per dir meglio ostruita dall'immaginaria traumaticità e « oscenità » della morte. Insomma è probabile che il dono dell'indeterminatezza — la facoltà che a ogni uomo è concessa, ma che non molti possono o sanno sfruttare sino all'ultimo, di vedere la morte sempre alla stessa distanza — non sia indispensabile soltanto per vivere senza tormento, ma anche per avvicinarsi con gioia alla morte. Si può assaporare la fine solo a patto di percepirla come un bene esiguo ma non contato, uno spazio breve e ultimo ma infinito. (Tutto questo prescinde, è chiaro, dai problemi « medici »; anzi, presuppone la loro soluzione. Mi sembra che la terapia del dolore e l'assistenza ai cosiddetti malati terminali siano fra le poche cose davvero serie di cui la scienza dovrebbe occuparsi a tempo pieno. Tenere in vita una persona può essere semplicemente un sopruso se quella che si tiene non è una persona e ciò dentro cui la si tiene non è, nella sua ultimità, una vita.)

Solo adesso comincio forse a intravedere il significato di un'immagine che da molti anni inesplicatamente nutro e mi nutre, quella di mio padre che dopo il primo attacco cardiaco (il secondo, pochi mesi dopo, lo avrebbe ucciso) se ne sta a letto, di buonissimo umore, ben appoggiato a due cuscini, e legge, legge ininterrottamente, legge o rilegge tutti i romanzi possibili . . . Rivedo le pile di libri sul comodino, l'azzurro dei vecchi Einaudi, il verde della « Romantica », il giallo dei Classiques Garnier . . . E ricordo la mia sorpresa, il mio superstizioso sgomento: perché leggere tanto, perché impadronirsi di tante storie, di tante verità se gli restava così poco tempo per « usarle », per metterle a profitto? Forse, pensavo, legge soltanto per « passare il tempo » . . . Ma

I've always thought that ultimity (I know there's no such word, but for the moment I'm not inclined to relinquish or replace it) is the most precious, the most intoxicating of all delicacies. But how can we consider it without fear? Someone condemned to death could be for one night the happiest man on earth if his happiness weren't covered over—or, more precisely, obstructed—by the imagined traumaticity and "obscenity" of death. After all, it's likely that the gift of indeterminateness—the faculty granted to every man, but one that few can or know how to exploit to the ultimate, to see death always at the same distance—is indispensable not only for living without torment, but also for drawing near to death with joy. We can savor the end only insofar as we perceive it as a slight but uncalculated good, a brief and ultimate but infinite space. (All of this, clearly, takes no account of "medical" problems; on the contrary, it presupposes their solution. It seems to me that pain therapy and helping the so-called terminally ill are among the few really serious things that science ought to be concerning itself with on a full-time basis. Keeping a person alive can be merely an abuse if what's being kept is not a person and what's being kept in it is not, in its ultimity, a life.)

Perhaps only now am I starting to glimpse the meaning of an image that for many years I have inexplicably nurtured and that has nurtured me, that of my father who after his first heart attack (his second, a few months later, killed him), stays in bed, in excellent spirits, well supported by a couple of pillows, and reads, reads uninterruptedly, reads and rereads every imaginable novel . . . Once again I see the piles of books on his night-table, the blue of the old Einaudi editions, the green of the Romantica series, the yellow of the Classiques Garnier . . . And I recall my surprise, my superstitious dismay: why read so much, why appropriate so many stories, so many truths if he had so little time left to "use" them, to profit from them? Maybe, I thought, he's reading only "to pass the time" . . . But

no: finito un libro, diceva sorridendo che era contento, che ne era « valsa la pena » . . . Ma come? era la mia stessa reazione — ma io avevo vent'anni, e se ero contento d'aver letto un nuovo libro o d'averne capito meglio uno che avevo letto troppo presto, con troppa foga e innocenza, era perché ogni volta mi sentivo un po' più forte, più ricco, perché sentivo di avere qualcosa in più da smerciare, da investire, da far fruttare nel corso del mio vergine e inesauribile futuro, a profitto del mio orgoglio e a edificazione del genere umano: *tempus aedificandi* . . . Beh, adesso comincio a capire — forse, più semplicemente, comincio a essere mio padre. Quest'anno lui avrebbe cento anni, l'anno prossimo io avrò la sua età, l'età di quando è morto. Se mi sono trascinato dietro, di casa in casa, tanti libri era, comincio a rendermene conto, per metterli un giorno o l'altro in pila — gli azzurri, i verdi, i gialli — sul comodino. A proposito, dovrei avere un comodino accanto al letto. Dovrei avere un letto, un vero letto — un letto con una spalliera di noce a cui appoggiare due cuscini. Non assaporo ancora, ma già immagino la gioia di accumulare silenziosamente dentro di me beni infruttiferi e intrasmissibili e sento che potrebbe essere la più pura, la più sottile, la più perfetta delle gioie.

C'entra? Non c'entra? Da un po' di tempo, se riesco a ricordare un sogno è con lo stesso misto di sollievo e di terrore con cui si pensa a uno scampato pericolo.

no: finishing a book, he smiled and said that he was content, that it was "worth the trouble" . . . How so? was my usual reaction—but I was twenty years old, and if I was content to have read a new book or to have better understood one that I had read too early, with too much ardor and innocence, it was because I felt a little stronger, a little richer every time, because I felt that I had something, moreover, to sell, to invest, to earn interest on in the course of my virgin and inexhaustible future, for the benefit of my pride and for the edification of humanity: *tempus aedificandi* . . . Well, now I'm starting to understand—perhaps, more simply, I'm starting to be my father. This year he would be a hundred years old, next year I will be his age, the age he was when died. If I have dragged so many books behind me, from house to house, it was, as I'm beginning to be aware, so that one day or another I could pile them—the blue, the green, the yellow—on the night-table. Speaking of which, I ought to have a night-table next to the bed. I ought to have a bed, a real bed—a bed with a walnut headboard against which to prop a couple of pillows. I'm not savoring it yet, but I'm already imagining the joy of accumulating silently within myself some non-interest-bearing and non-negotiable assets and I feel that it could be the purest, the subtlest, the most perfect of all joys.

Relevant? Irrelevant? Lately, if I'm able to remember a dream it's with the same mixture of relief and terror with which one thinks about a danger that's been avoided.

Mi sembra di vivere sottovuoto
in una strana terra di nessuno
senza suoni né odori
andando avanti e indietro inutilmente
come un animale cattivo,
respirando per antica abitudine
un'aria resa irrespirabile
dalla sua totale innaturalezza
più ancora che dai veleni. Che c'entri
anche il fatto che all'1 di via Revere
o dalla sua Urbino al telefono
ha smesso raggiungermi la voce
sapida d'amarezza
e d'epica, contagiosa allegria
dell'amico trovato per ventura
e per colmo di sventura perduto
nell'età degli ultimi amici, quando
per degli altri forse non c'è più tempo
e sicuramente non c'è più cuore?
Paolo, mi sogno a volte di dirgli
credendolo di colpo
all'altro capo d'un filo, è finita,
nessun battaglia da vincere
e neanche da combattere
con qualche promessa d'onore
in questo infrequentabile millennio,
moriremo tutti, come temevi,
berlusconiani . . . Ma di là
mi risponde un silenzio sanguinoso,
un lieve, solenne pulsare
soavemente percussivo
d'ali o d'acque o di fronde così simile,

I feel as if I'm living in a vacuum
in a peculiar no man's land
with neither sounds nor smells,
uselessly just going back and forth
like a savage animal,
breathing only out of an old habit
an air that has been made unbreathable
through its absolute unnaturalness
more than if by poison. How does it bear
on the matter that his voice no longer comes
to me at 1 Via Revere or from
his Urbino on the telephone,
savory with bitterness
and with an epic and contagious joy,
the voice of a friend found by pure good fortune
and lost by the extremity of misfortune
in this, the age of last friends, when
maybe there isn't time for any others
and certainly there isn't any heart?
Paolo, I sometimes dream of telling him,
suddenly believing that he's there
on the other end of the line, it's over now,
there are no more battles left to win,
there isn't even one to fight
with some pledge of honor
in this infrequentable millennium,
we're all going to die, just as you feared,
as Berlusconians . . . But from beyond
a sanguinary silence answers me,
a solemn faint pulsation
softly percussive
of wings or water or leaves uncannily,

m’accorgerò più tardi,
a quello delle sue psicomachie,
dei suoi ritmi francescani, frenetici.

as I will later realize,
reminiscent of his psychomachies,
of his Franciscan and frenetic rhythms.

Allo stadio andavamo presto,
non volevamo perdere
la partita prima della partita.
In campo, uguali da confonderli
a dei giocatori veri, i ragazzi
delle squadre chiamate primavera.
Guardarli era una pura meraviglia.
Forse perché correvano sul prato
con furibonda leggerezza
come se fosse, quello che facevano,
davvero un gioco — o forse
perché l'altra cosa, la vera,
doveva ancora cominciare,
era ancora tutta davanti a noi
con le sue ombre sanguinose,
con il suo cupo carico di gloria.

We went to the stadium early,
we didn't want to miss
the match before the match.
On the field, enough like them
to be taken for the real players,
the boys of the junior teams.
They were a pure marvel to watch.
Maybe because they ran across
the grass with furious lightness
as if what they were doing was
a real game—or maybe because
the other thing, the real one,
hadn't yet begun,
was still all before us,
with its bloody shadows,
with its dark load of glory.

La piazza

1

Mi piace questa piazza. Più è deserta
e più mi piace. Posso popolarla
di chi voglio, incontrarci, camminando,
gli altrimenti introvabili.
C'è mio padre che pure, a quanto so,
da queste parti non c'è mai venuto
ma sembra contento di passeggiare
(lui diceva, mi ricordo, *flâner*)
sotto i portici, o di scrutare
l'interminabile crepuscolo
seduto a un tavolino del caffè
fumando lentamente
una delle sue Turmac con il filtro.
C'è mia madre, molto più giovane
di quando m'ha lasciato (dai vestiti
si direbbe persino che la guerra
debba ancora scoppiare):
sta aspettando l'autobus, forse,
o forse invece guarda i manifesti
della stagione di prosa, stupita
da tutti quegli attori e quelle attrici
che non ha mai sentito nominare.
E c'è, appena in ritardo, mio fratello
al volante d'una vecchia MG
(sì, per lui si può fare un'eccezione,
aprire per un attimo al passato

The Square

1

I like this square. The emptier it is
the more I like it. I can populate it
with anyone I want to, meeting up on foot
with those who are otherwise nowhere to be found.
There's my father, who, as far as I know,
was never in this area in his life
and yet he seems content to be strolling by
(his word for it, I remember, was *flâner*)
under the porticos, or else to be
peering deeply into the endless twilight
while sitting at a little table of
an outdoor café and slowly
smoking another one of his filtered Turmacs.
There's my mother, so much younger than
she was the day she went away from me
(and from the way she's dressed it seems the war
still hasn't broken out):
maybe she's waiting for the bus to come
or maybe on the other hand she's looking
at the posters for the theater season,
astonished by the names of all the actors
and actresses that she has never heard of.
And there's my brother, just a little bit late,
sitting behind the wheel of an old MG
(yes, for him an exception can be made,
opening up a pedestrian zone for just

l'isola pedonale),
così magro, così bello, un ragazzo
di cinquant'anni! e vedo che sorride,
che mi fa segno con la mano
come a dire « ci vediamo più tardi »
ma con l'aria di volersene andare,
di voler proseguire già stasera
per dove fa più caldo o c'è più neve.

2

Oppure ecco di colpo le tue gambe
meravigliose sui primi tacchi alti
della tua adolescenza.
Ti spio fra una colonna e l'altra, è fuori,
è alla gran luce che cammini, svelta
e indolente, dandoti arie
d'avere i sedici anni
che non avrai che a maggio. Come sbanda
per tenere il tuo passo vittorioso,
con che delizia s'affatica
di decennio in decennio
a inseguirti fin dove non c'è traccia
né di me né di noi
la mia smodata tenerezza.

a moment into the past),
so slender, so good-looking, a young lad
of fifty! and I see that he is smiling,
signaling to me with his hand
as if to say "We'll see each other later"
but with an air of wanting to be gone,
already heading this evening for a place
where it's warmer or where there's more snow.

2

Or else all of a sudden here are your
two marvelous legs atop the first high heels
of your adolescence.
Between one column and another one
I watch you: it's outside in the wide light
you're walking, quickly and indifferently,
giving yourself the airs
of the sixteen years that won't be yours till May.
As my intemperate affection swerves
to keep apace of your triumphant stride,
with what delight it strives
to follow you through decade after decade
to where there isn't
any trace of either me or us.

da VERSI DISPERSI E D'OCCASIONE
(*da* L'OPERA POETICA, 2006)

from UNCOLLECTED AND OCCASIONAL POEMS
(*from* THE POETICAL WORKS, 2006)

I giorni della Terra Santa

Quando soffia l'inverno e il vento porta
campane d'arsenico bianco ai rami secchi degli alberi
Cristo siede in silenzio nel sepolcro.

Quando la primavera spacca gli occhi dell'erba
e le gemme tagliano e sorridono come coltelli
Cristo siede in silenzio nel sepolcro.

Quando l'estate spezza col suo bastone d'oro
le ginocchia e le reni agli animali
Cristo siede in silenzio nel sepolcro.

Quando l'autunno apre le mani sul prati
e schiaccia le lucertole e affonda le pietre
Cristo siede in silenzio nel sepolcro.

(1950)

The Days of the Holy Land

When winter blows gusts and the wind brings bells
of white arsenic to the dry branches of the trees
Christ sits in silence in the sepulcher.

When springtime cracks the eyes of grass wide open
and the buds cut and smile like blades of knives
Christ sits in silence in the sepulcher.

When summer smashes with its golden club
the knees and even the backs of animals
Christ sits in silence in the sepulcher.

When autumn spreads its hands above the meadows
and crushes lizards and capsizes stones
Christ sits in silence in the sepulcher.

(1950)

Autunno in campagna. Inverno in città

Siamo stati fra gli ultimi a tornare:
anche il giorno dei morti si sta bene in campagna
se non attacca a piovere. E l'autunno è sembrato
così dolce quest'anno, nella casa
coperta d'ipoteche e già venduta
al fornaio di buon cuore. La ghiaia che sprofonda
nel viale — la campana suonerà
quattro volte ancòra, cinque? Quel che importa è partire
a stagione finita, con la nebbia,
rimandando il dolore a primavera.

Autumn in the Country. Winter in the City

We were among the last ones to go back:
even All Souls' Day is pleasant out in the country
if it doesn't start to rain. And autumn seemed
to be so mild this year, here in the house
covered with mortgages and already sold
to the goodhearted baker. The gravel that gives way
along the path—the bell will ring another
four times, or maybe five? What's important is to leave
when the season's over, with the mist,
putting off the sorrow till the spring.

Preghiera particolare

È il mio sogno più cupo: sparire nella folla
dei peccatori, fitta e silenziosa
come una migrazione di sardine.
E so che dopo più nessuno
potrà tirarmi fuori, né sapere
qual è mio nome.
                    Signore, il mio nome
è la parola della Maddalena
in San Giovanni 20,16. Se vuoi
ricordalo, per poco
che lo meriti il cuore.

Private Prayer

This is my darkest dream: to disappear
into the crowd of sinners, densely packed
and silent as a migration of sardines.
And I know that afterwards nobody will
be able to pull me out of it again,
or know what my name is.
O Lord, my name
is the word spoken by the Magdalene
in John 20:16. If it be your will
remember it, however little
my heart deserves it.

Esplanade

I vecchi che nel riquadro della porta arrancano — e le vecchie
gli uni e le altre con bastoni
componibili, snodati, retrattili
più uno che troppo forte, da sordo
discuteva col cuoco
m'ammoniscono: basta,
basta, sta' quieto. Ma sì,
certo . . . Infilo i bastoni dei giornali
nei loro loculi di noce
attento a non incrinare il guscio d'uovo del sonno
prima che il sonno abbia le ali
come se fossi uno di loro, collezionisti di vertebre, assassini
promossi a moribondi per anzianità di servizio.

(1971)

Esplanade

The old men who hobble in the doorframe—and the old women,
both bunches of them with their sectional,
articulated, retractable walking sticks,
plus one man who too loudly, because of deafness,
was arguing with the chef,
admonish me: enough,
enough, be quiet. Oh yes,
of course . . . I slide the sticks for the newspapers
into their walnut burial niches
being careful not to crack the eggshell of sleep
before sleep has its wings
as if I were one of them, collectors of vertebrae, killers
promoted to death's door for length of service.

(1971)

Bisogna saperlo, Cristo non amava
gli omosessuali e gli adulteri. Lo leggo nei giornali
del 14/5/85, l'ha detto il papa in un suo viaggio.
Forse, mi dico, non amava neanche
gli storpi, i ciechi, i lebbrosi,
i paralitici, quelli che non sanno nuotare,
forse era questo che scriveva
col dito nella polvere
(San Giovanni 8,6) senza pensare
che il suo vicario, dopo venti secoli,
con la sua forte vista da sciatore
l'avrebbe decifrato.

You need to realize, Christ didn't love
homosexuals and adulterers. So I see from the papers
of 5/14/85, the pope said so on one of his travels.
Maybe, I think, he didn't even love
the halt, the blind, the lepers,
the paralytics, people who can't swim,
maybe that's what he wrote
with his finger in the dust
(John, chapter 8, verse 6) without thinking
that his vicar, after twenty centuries,
with the keen and powerful vision of a skier,
would have deciphered it.

La navetta spaziale esplosa in volo il 28 gennaio 1986

Che povero lutto, mormoro
a chissà chi, chissà in che lingua,
davanti alla televisione che s'inceppa
su una traiettoria di fuoco, su una forca di fumo,
che povero lutto per una morte
così sontuosa, luccicante . . .
Neanche un imperatore, neanche un dio
è mai sparito in tanta gloria,
sotto gli occhi atterriti
di tanti sudditi o fedeli . . . Eppure
(non mi esce dalla testa:
un trito, triste ritornello ormai)
che povero lutto, che povero lutto!
Per un'ora, sapremo,
è caduta una pioggia di lamiere,
di scorie, di faville,
resti di macchina, di macchinazione . . .
Ma sulla terra, intanto, poche lacrime
in diretta, asciugate in fretta, con pudore,
madri e sorelle subito impietrite
in un sogno d'orgoglio . . .
Ah Cristo, vorrei dire (e per un attimo
mi viene in mente, amaramente,
che così, Crista, si chiamava lei,
la settima vittima, la maestrina, spedita
a far lezione d'orgoglio nello spazio),
Cristo, vorrei gridare, non è questo,
non può essere questo il vostro sogno,

The Space Shuttle Explodes in Flight, January 28, 1986

What poor mourning, I murmur,
to who knows whom, and who knows in what language
sitting before the television jammed
on a trajectory of fire, a pitchfork of smoke,
what poor mourning for so sumptuous,
so glittering a death . . .
Not even an emperor, not even a god
has ever disappeared in so much glory,
before the horrified eyes
of so many subjects or devotees . . . And yet
(I can't get it out of my head:
by now a trite and trivial sad refrain)
what poor mourning, what poor mourning!
For an hour, we know,
a rain has been coming down, a rain of slag,
of sparks, of sheet metal,
remains of machinery, of machination . . .
But on the earth, in the meantime, a few tears
shown live, and quickly dried, with modesty,
mothers and sisters swiftly petrified
in a dream of pride . . .
Ah Christ, I want to say (and for an instant
it comes piercingly to mind
that Christa was the name
of the seventh victim, the young teacher who
was sent into space to give lessons of pride),
Christ, I want to cry out, this is not,
this cannot be your dream,

la nazione che vince in pace e in guerra,
l'onniscienza della scienza, l'onnipotenza del potere . . .
No, vorrei dire a quella gente muta,
sognate i *vostri* sogni, piangete la *vostra* morte.

the nation that is triumphant in peace and war,
the omniscience of science, the omnipotence of power . . .
No, I want to say to that hushed people,
dream *your* own dreams, and weep for *your* own death.

Sera del 27 gennaio 1897

Cammino alla ventura. L'oliveto
m'è come un popolo afflitto e convulso.
Lascio parlare l'anima agli olivi.
Tutto quello che accade non accade
se non tra l'albero e me, se non tra l'erba
e me, se non tra me e la gleba. Il vespro
s'infolta illune. Qualcuno ricomincia
a lottare con l'angelo . . .

Evening of January 27, 1897

I walk round randomly. The olive grove
seems a distressed, convulsive crowd of people.
I let my spirit speak to the olive trees.
Everything that happens doesn't happen
if not between the tree and me, the grass
and me, me and the sod. The evening thickens
moonless. Someone's beginning once again
to wrestle with the angel . . .

Ma quante volte glielo devo dire
di dargli requie, requie eterna? (Scendo
sempre di più nella stima della luce
eppure, vedi, eccomi ancora a credere
che sia per altri che devo pregarlo
di questo o di quello, per loro,
gli inermi, i senza guscio . . . Chissà quando
avrò il coraggio di farlo per me,
d'arredarla a mio modo la cabina
sulla Caronte, l'arca
del passato futuro . . .)

But how often must I tell him to
give someone rest, eternal rest? (I keep
going lower in the estimate of light,
and yet, you see, here I am still believing
that it's for others I must pray to him,
for this one or for that one, for all those
defenseless ones, with no shell . . . Who knows when
I'll have the courage to do it for myself,
to rig the cabin out in my own style
on the *Charon*, the ark
of future past . . .)

Il fruttivendolo pugliese
famoso nel quartiere
perché teneva aperto anche d'agosto
se n'è andato, non so se all'altro mondo
o alle Seychelles o alle Maldive,
comunque a godersi il meritatissimo
frutto del suo sudore.
A tutt'oggi il buco del suo negozio
non è stato otturato
e così quel tratto di via Tadino
dove Clemente Rebora ha abitato
prima di farsi prete
ha qualcosa d'incerto, d'incompiuto,
di malinconicamente esitante
come il sorriso d'uno sdentato.

The Apulian greengrocer
renowned in the neighborhood
because his shop was open even in August
has gone away, I don't know whether to
the next world, or the Maldives or Seychelles,
to enjoy at any rate the richly earned
fruit of the sweat of his brow.
To this day they still haven't filled up
the open hole of his store
and so that stretch of Via Tadino
where Clemente Rebora lived before
he became a priest
has something irresolute and incomplete,
sadly hesitant about it, like the smile
of someone missing one of his front teeth.

Un uomo, dunque, può essere felice
anzi estasiato, « ecstatic », così ho letto
sul giornale di oggi,
della morte di altri uomini, compreso
un ragazzino di quattordici anni,
massacrati ad personam
a raffiche di missili e bazooka
e di questo non solo esser felice
nell'inviolabile buio del cuore
ma dirsi tale, proclamarsi tale
alla luce del sole
e senza una parola di pietà?
E può, quest'uomo che è così felice
e così brutalmente
si proclama felice, essere il capo
cristiano d'una nazione cristiana
che vuole imporre il bene a tutto il mondo?
Domande senza risposta, domande
del 22 luglio 2003.

So then, is it possible for a man to be
happy, indeed "ecstatic," as I see
in the newspaper today,
about the deaths of other men, including
a fourteen-year-old boy, the lot of them
massacred *ad personam*
by an assault of missiles and bazookas,
and not just to be happy over it
in the inviolable darkness of his heart
but to say so, to publicly proclaim it
out in the light of the sun
and without one single syllable of compassion?
And is it possible for this man, who is
so happy and who proclaims
his happiness so brutally, to be
the Christian leader of a Christian nation
intent on imposing good on the whole world?
Questions without an answer, questions for
July the twenty-second, 2003.

On "The Wedding"

The poem is entitled "The Wedding," it's one of the most recent that I've written, it's in four parts, it's a poem that has a story which, afterwards, I'll try to briefly recount and which calls for a few initial clarifications.

Therefore, I'll divide my attempt at explanation into two parts: a preliminary one, with a few essential pieces of information, and one a bit more protracted after the reading.

I can provide the initial clarifications by reading the note I've written for the poem, which is going to appear in the book I'm about to publish.

The note reads: "Of the four sections of 'The Wedding' the first three are based to a large extent on the famous painting by Jan van Eyck known as *The Arnolfini Spouses* or *The Arnolfini Wedding*, probably a double portrait of the Luccan merchant Giovanni Arnolfini and his wife Giovanna, now in the National Gallery in London, while the principal references in the last part relate, although in a somewhat arbitrary manner, to another painting by the same artist, now lost, as it can be seen or imagined in a picture by Wilhelm van Haecht that reproduces the gallery of an Antwerp art collector in 1615."

The note may seem to obscure more than it clarifies, but it's very important to understand, before the reading, that the poem takes place within this very famous painting and with a final reference to another painting. Afterwards, I'll try to explain all of this.

The Wedding

I have no grand pretensions. I content myself
with being be the man dressed in blue, or red, who is reflected
between back and back, unfocused, softly
fungible—the blue one
or the red, it doesn't matter
which—
in the lobed wheel of the Passion.
Johannes fuit hic. Not
in his albino look,
in the wax hand that is touching your hand.

Then there are no windows in the bridal chamber.
Or

the narrow, crooked white strip, the gold
of rachitic apples that rises,
cold, from the invisible *campiello* . . .
With thin

waxy phalanges he preaches, arranges
the consumption of the velvets, the future
position of the skeletons.

Never in one place so many Giovannis—under
headgear of cloth, of beaver fur
and silks, and haughty turbans—for a single
spasm of moonlight or dawn
of which, you pray, not one
drop will spill
on the polished floor
or descend, a ribbon of blood,
to encircle your throat
till life do you part.

Alone, now, in the disproportion of your hair
on your smooth and slim bare torso, on your funereal throat,
you wipe your belly, you sway
like a chalice or a flute between the handmaid and the basin,
firm, upright, tenderly
woman further below the waist
and neither, I think, do you perceive the serpents
that lick the oval of your nipples,
all of it far from your mind while waiting
for what has been.

So, I'll begin by recounting the background of the poem, which is as follows: this painting has greatly fascinated me—as it has, I believe, everyone who has seen it or, in any case, many of those who have seen it—and for a long time I have had it in mind to set a poem in it; not to write a poem about it, but to set a poem in it, to try to get inside the painting.

Why? Because I was fascinated by a combination of things; I was fascinated by this couple, so very young or perhaps without any age at all; I was fascinated by the motif of the mirror: you'll recall that in the painting, behind the pair of newlyweds, of presumable newlyweds, there's a round mirror in which there are the reflections of two people who have come into the room, and it appears that one of them is the painter himself, van Eyck.

Then there is the famous problem or enigma—or to some extent considered such—of the writing on the mirror, which says "Johannes fuit hic."

The thing seemed so strange that for a long time it was read as "Johannes fecit hoc"; instead, what is actually written there is "fuit hic"; thus it isn't merely a signature; it is, it seems, testimony to the fact that the painter was involved as a witness to the wedding that he then portrayed.

These figures are out of focus, one dressed in red and one in blue; no one knows, in fact, which of the two is the painter, it could be either one of them. They're the two witnesses; one is also the artist.

Then there's the curious fact that everyone in this painting is named Giovanni: the merchant Arnolfini is named Giovanni, his wife is named Giovanna, the painter is named Giovanni. My name is Giovanni.

I have carried with me, within me, the fascination of this painting and the desire to create something from it, to enter into it in some way, for many years, as I've told you; and yet always with a vague desire, a vague intention.

Then, last year, two things happened that brought this intention back to the surface. One was rather external: I reread Tolstoy's *Anna Karenina*, which is in its way, as you know, a book about marriage, and I was struck by a fact to which I had never paid attention, that Anna Karenina's husband and lover have the same name; and so that business about the names came back into my mind.

The other, more decisive thing that roused the project within me and put it back into circulation is that someone who had become very dear to me in that period put me in mind of the female figure in *The Arnolfini Wedding* and, in general, the female type in van Eyck's paintings.

This fact acted as an intermediary between this picture, the double portrait of the Arnolfinis, and the other picture that I mention in the note, which, to complicate things a little, is a lost painting, one that can be seen in another painting that depicts a collection of paintings. In this second picture there's a figure that I have arbitrarily superimposed upon, or made to correspond to, the female figure in the principal painting, *The Arnolfini Wedding*.

What was born out of all this I am not entirely certain; there was born a series of triangulations among the figures portrayed, the supposed figure of the creator of the painting—the paintings, rather—and myself; there was born this sort of a trilogy plus one, a trilogy plus a piece, of the wedding, of the couple, of the connection between life and death that is implied by the joining of two people in this way. It is from here, I believe, that all the images in the poem originate.

Looking at it part by part, the first, which begins "I have no grand pretensions . . . ," is the moment at which there is a sort of identification of roles; the speaker identifies, or pretends to identify, with the creator of the painting, and from this comes "I content myself with being the man dressed in blue, or red"—that is, the two figures seen in the mirror, of whom one may be, and probably is, the painter.

The lobed wheel of passion that is spoken of is the mirror, which, as I recall, has a frame of lobes; within the lobes, extremely small, scenes from the passion of Christ are represented.

Always in the first part, beyond the speaker's identification with one of the figures in the mirror, there is an identification of a grammatical type.

The male figure, who is the merchant Arnolfini, becomes identified with a third person singular; therefore, "his albino look" is related to him, while the female figure is identified with a *your* ("your hand").

Thus, there is an *I* who is or pretends to be the author of the painting, there is a *he* who is the groom and there is a *you* who is the bride.

In the second part as I understand it the principal theme is of a claustrophobic character: the nuptial chamber comes to be seen as a closed space, without the slightest opening ("the narrow, crooked white strip," etc.), and as a place no one gets out of again; the nuptial chamber is a place where positions are fixed once and for all, and thus the groom's gesture ("waxy phalanges," etc.) seems to arrange a future until death ("arranges / the consumption of the velvets, the future / position of the skeletons,") as if from that moment on it were indeed impossible to get out of there again.

In the third part the theme of the proliferation of all the people with the same name ("Never in one place so many Giovannis") is put in evidence; it seems to me that the meaning is the ambiguity, the circulation, through the various figures, of a single essence.

Then there is the theme of the light, which was already touched on in the second part, the light that filters into the closed space of the nuptial chamber; and, frankly, I wouldn't know what more to say.

The fourth part tries to connect the main image, that of the spouses and their wedding and the afterlife of their marriage, with the other painting.

The other painting (the lost painting) depicts a naked woman who is drying herself next to a washbasin and a maidservant. This seems to me to be an attempt to create an after and even a before in relation to the main picture. The scene of the naked woman who is drying herself, and who is identified with the bride in *The Arnolfini Wedding*, is perceived as contemporaneously preceding and following the scene of the wedding; this explains the final oxymoron, the "waiting for what has been": the repetition of this act, of this ritual, is repetition and therefore not time.

I'll stop here for now, taking for granted all that's been said in these days, which is that the explanations a poet can give are much more in fact than in law and are very rarely theoretically based.

I can say how the poem came to be. A bit *a posteriori*, I've tried to see what themes I think emerge from it. But it may be the case that readers see other ones, and I would be happy to be able to confirm, or not, the plausibility of other interpretations.

The above is a translation of a talk given by Giovanni Raboni at a conference at the Sapienza University of Rome in February 1982.

"To Live at Least at Fifty Percent": The *Poesia* Interview with Giovanni Raboni (January 2003) conducted by Daniele Piccini

I met with Giovanni Raboni at various times in the lobby of the Hotel Diana Majestic, in the neighborhood of Porta Venezia, a short distance from his home in Milan. As a background to our conversations, free and wandering recollections in which Raboni reconstructed the story of his life step by step (from his childhood to his earliest cultural development, up to the emotional and intellectual events of his mature years), the sounds of plates, glasses, and voices were scattered through the spacious glass- and mirror-filled surroundings. In meeting after meeting, it seemed to me that behind the poet's eyes was an unexpected mosaic, composed of numerous facets and refractions, in which the story of a man was in the end indistinguishable, as it should be, from his cultural and poetic activities. An induced self-portrait, if I may call it that, which maintains, for one who has had the chance to assemble it, a resonant confabulatory echo: the tone of a revision, quiet and at ease, of the double entry of life. A biographical and cultural reconstruction, offered now to readers and scholars in the hope that it will serve, as a postscript and an instrument of orientation, to further their understanding of that extremely rich and varied body of poetry that the author has entrusted to our comprehension.

The principal location of your life and also of your poetry is Milan: what do you remember about the city as you saw it in your childhood years?
I have to give this subject some background: Milan is doubly my city, in that I was born here and I lived here for a few years, more or less until the third grade, if I remember correctly, and then there was the parenthesis of the war and the evacuation when, after the first time the city was bombarded, we went away to a house in the country near Varese, where I spent the rest of the war. The period of the evacuation was an especially long and important one for me, and it created an absolute break with the past. Then, when I went back to Milan, I rediscovered it: living in this city was a new emotion for me, in that I had erased the emotions of childhood; also, because as very young children we live more in a neighborhood than a city, and this return was a very strong emotion in that I really fell in love with the city. That's why my association with Milan is a double one. So my memories of Milan aren't of childhood, but mostly of adolescence, and they're memories of postwar Milan.

Where did you live?

I was born in Porta Venezia, in Via San Gregorio, and I lived there before and just after the war, until I got married and left that neighborhood to live in other parts of the city, in the old town; then, by choice, I came back here. This is one part of the city that's preserved its architectural appearance, unlike other areas that are totally unrecognizable today: despite being near the main railroad station, which was more frequently bombed, this neighborhood was strangely spared, unlike the old town, for example, where the Duomo itself had been a target. My house wasn't destroyed, I left it then, but it still exists today, and the whole neighborhood still has its character, even though it's been turned into a bit of a "ghetto," housing a lot of immigrants. It's an area that I like very much, because it has its own, I won't say night life, but its own night presence. When I happen to go through the old town at night, I feel a kind of sensation of death, just because there's nobody there and everything is closed.

Is Milan today very different from what you remember of the city from your adolescence?

There's a huge difference, even if over time I may have mythologized the city of those years, but as I recall there was a curiosity about everything and a great intellectual vivacity that lasted, with alternating phases, more or less until 1968. That date really marked a dividing line, after which the publishing and cultural sector went through major changes, with a gradual loss of vitality. It's odd that when people talk about the crisis of intellectual life and particularly with reference to Milan, they almost never recollect one fact that to me is decisive, which is that the publishers no longer have their offices within the fabric of the city. Mondadori's move from Via Bianca di Savoia to Segrate and Bompiani's move from Via Pascane have been tremendously significant. Those publishing houses were very important gathering places, the intellectuals met there: you went to Mondadori, for example, not on business but to wait for Vittorio Sereni to come out, you went there to say hello to him, or because you knew that Giacomo Di Benedetti would be there because he was passing through Milan. The publisher's office was really a place where you went to meet people. Nowadays all this isn't possible anymore, partly for practical reasons, because it's very inconvenient to go to Segrate, and partly because it no longer means anything, given that certain rituals that used to be current are gone now: the custom of having a drink with someone, of having dinner together. After their relocation the publishers became less important as centers of cultural life.

Who are the people you principally recall from the period right after the war?
More than in the years just after the war, because then I was still a boy looking at things from the outside, my memories go back to when I started to spend time in this world. From that period I particularly recall Sereni, Vittorini, Enzio Paci, who were my masters and my friends.

Can you tell me about your complex and intense friendship with Sereni?
I really did have a very strong friendship with Vittorio Sereni, thanks to his talent for befriending me at once. We met when I was very young: I hadn't taken my high-school finals yet. I met him when he was the private tutor of a friend of mine, one that I went to Parini High School with for a few years and that I studied for finals with. After the war my academic career was very irregular: I didn't manage to go to school for more than two or three months at a time, probably as a result of the long "war vacation" following the evacuation. After that period I'd gotten out of the habit of going to school, then I promptly enrolled, but—either I got sick or I thought I was sick—I rarely attended, even though I'd never skipped any school years, I very rarely went to school. I somehow managed to get through all the subjects on my own, the only one I had to repeat was mathematics. With this friend then, who later went into publishing, I studied for a few exams, and since he took private lessons from Sereni, I had a means of meeting Vittorio, who quickly displayed his extraordinary capacity for offering friendship.

But had you already actively involved yourself in poetry, I mean to say, were you writing it?
Unfortunately, I'm a disgracefully precocious poet, very early on I felt the impulse to make "verse" like the poets I read. I started writing poetry when I was ten or even earlier: things I later burned. I think I had a good ear, even though those things were imitations, given that I had a read a great deal starting when I was very young: in a word, which isn't strictly true, I could say that I read everything during the war years. I read a great deal of poetry, a lot of novels, whether I understood everything or not, especially the novels, because understanding them required some life experience. In those years, when I was twelve, thirteen years old, I read so much. I remember even having devoured all of Shakespeare, in the Sansoni edition that came out in 1944–45. I flung myself ravenously on that edition, reading it through from the first page to the last. I was an omnivorous and unconscious reader, with a passion that swept away even incomprehension. Those were my years in Sant'Ambrogio (between Varese and the Sacred Mount), the years of the evacuation.

How did the books you read reach you at Sant'Ambrogio?
Some books came to Varese, and then my father came back from Milan every day and brought a few books with him. My whole family had this great passion for books, we had a family library and I remember that they said about my grandfather, my father's father, whom I never knew, that he never came home in the evening without going past the bookstore and buying at least one book. So there was no way that this passion for reading wouldn't have been passed on to me as well.

Which poets impressed you in those early days?
I read in sequence the poets of the late nineteenth and the twentieth century, moved by a passion for Pascoli and D'Annunzio, which I still have. I read books of poetry with the passion of an imitator, of one, that is, who wanted to write in his turn, while for the novel I had a disinterested passion, that of a reader exclusively. With novels I could separate the pleasure of reading from the anxiety to emulate, which I felt in connection with poetry. So for me the pleasure of reading was really embodied by novels; poetry was more of a hand-to-hand combat.

Do you still have this relationship of anxious emulation with poetry?
No, I don't have it anymore, because I know I have my own road marked out, but still, reading poets is never an experience of pure pleasure, because the critical impulse always follows.

Were you already reading Proust at Sant'Ambrogio?
No, I read him a bit later, because my father advised me to read him when I felt I was at a level where I could take on the original text. I can even say exactly when I encountered Proust, because I read his work, all of it, in the summer after my graduation: it was the present that my father gave me just after my final exams and that I've kept to this day like a relic. It was the summer of 1950: the Einaudi translation was already out, but I didn't read that.

So the Sant'Ambrogio years were important even for the cultural aspect. What was your life like otherwise in that period, under the constellation of the war?
At first I lived those years like a splendid adventure, because Sant'Ambrogio was a place where you went in the summer. The lack of a schedule, the spectacle of the changing seasons, plus the legitimization of not going to school, turned everything into a sort of huge vacation. I remember those first years with a sense of adventure and freedom. Then, however, they began the first

heavy bombardments of Milan, which came to us chiefly through the accounts my father gave. Then followed the evolving political events of September 8, before which I don't recall having had any political feelings. After that crucial day a few of my friends who wanted to flee to Switzerland began leaving, and the first news of the partisans began circulating. At that point my father, who until that moment had been neither a fascist nor an antifascist, took a political position. After the German occupation he had to flee and abandon his job; he was a high-ranking official in the Milan city government. He took some definite positions against the fortification of Milan, since this was being talked about, that is, defending Milan from the eventual arrival of the Allies. He held some opposing views, and so he fled Milan and for a short while he lived the experience of being underground, like some of his friends. I remember having lived the last years, from 1943 on, even though I was still a little boy, with a certain awareness of what was going on, an awareness of dangers, from listening to the news on Radio London, for example. I lived through the end of the war and the Liberation with a certain maturity. After the war, then, my father returned to Milan, reinstated by the Committee of National Liberation, he resumed his duties as a general secretary, the highest possible career grade in the city government. Thanks to my father's job I lived those years after the war, the years of reconstruction, a little bit from the inside, in the sense that I knew what was going on: the first socialist mayors, for example.

There isn't much of this wartime experience in your poetry, except for the late recollections of Verses of War and Love *(1990), at least until the very recent* Glimmers of History *(2002) . . .*
No, in fact, though something may have come out then, but at a distance, not then and there. The first things that I consider mature date from the very early fifties, when I was seventeen, eighteen years old, and they show the effects of my post-war discovery of English-language poetry, namely Pound and Eliot, who were crucial for me; up to that point I'd been devoted solely to Italian poetry: D'Annunzio, Pascoli, Montale, Ungaretti were the poets that inspired me and that I was imitating. From my reading of Eliot, combined with that of Pound, I developed a mechanism of disguise into which the autobiographical persona disappeared.

Did this kind of suppression amount to a choice on your part?
I can't say precisely. While there was the appeal of objectivity in that kind of poetry, which was somewhat contrary to how I had understood and lived poetry up to that point—that is, as lyric subjectivity, as confession—and since

I had nothing to confess, given my youth, my poetry around the age of fifteen was a poetry of imitation and lyrical outbursts. Later I moved from this kind of writing to an object-narrative kind, which probably concealed and didn't give voice to my teenage problems, fortunately, I think, given that I don't much care for teenage poetry, and from this perspective I don't even care for all of Rimbaud, though I do like the Rimbaud of the *Illuminations*. So, I avoided this phase by means of a literary-cultural construct and I didn't start talking about myself until much later.

In your earliest personal pieces the theme of death emerges, especially of your father and mother . . .
Yes, but these pieces already come later, and anyway even in these early efforts I'm more of a spectator.

In what sense and in what direction do you think the work of Pound and Eliot has influenced you?
I really believe in the search for an absolute objective correlative, as Eliot himself says.

In Eliot there wasn't even, as there is on the other hand in Montale, a strict correlation between object and symbol, there was really only the object . . .
Yes, there was only the object, the appeal of narrative, of poetry that describes, even though when I now reread the poems of those years, in which I was convinced that I was a follower of Eliot, I realize that Montale's influence is quite visible, especially in *The Unhealthiness of the Air* (1963), a chapbook that you can't find anymore, not even in libraries, but only in the antiquarian market.

Did that collection go into The Houses of the Vetra *(1966) largely intact, or did you make substantial changes there?*
I took some things out, I rearranged, some things I may have rewritten, but not that much.

Do you remember your father's death?
It was a terrible trauma. My father died in 1952, a year after my high school graduation, when I was in my first year at the university. It was, I repeat, a real trauma, because he was one of those fathers that a person feels he can count on, and I thought of my future as something that he would have taken care of. It was an enormous change, because with my father's death we had to solve a series of practical and financial problems, and because, nearly two

years later, my mother also died. We lived on my father's salary, and after his death we found ourselves with a pension that was much less than his regular pay, so we suddenly had to deal with problems of income. We had to leave and then sell the house in the country, which was our only property, because we rented the house in Milan: the Italian custom of buying a house—which I myself then picked up, in that I bought a house with my first wife, my second, and the woman I live with now—wasn't yet widespread among the middle class in those years, which we were a part of. There wasn't the urge to invest in buying a house, people used what they earned to lead a comfortable and proper life, so they lived in rental housing and stayed in the same place for twenty or thirty years.

Did your father's death influence your academic choices or had you decided to study law in any event?
I had decided to pursue law in any event. If anything, if my father had lived, I wouldn't have immediately looked for work after graduation, I might have wanted to stay in school for graduate study, and I might have tried an academic career. Another thing I might have liked to do, which I gave up because of the same financial problems, was a career in the judiciary. For the rest I was able to finish my education without a setback, as was my brother, who was five years older than me and earned a degree in architecture, thanks to help from rich relatives.

You said that, against your wishes, you started working immediately after graduation. What did you do?
I was hired by the legal department of a corporation. For about two years I worked for an oil company called San Quirico that was owned by a cousin of my father's, dealing with legal issues.

If I'm not mistaken, you're a graduate of the State University of Milan.
Yes, I graduated from State with a thesis on Roman jurisprudence.

Considering the voracious passion for literature that you spoke of earlier, didn't the choice of a different course of studies create an inner conflict in you?
To tell the truth, no. I've always had a very strong and clear sense that I should keep the two things distinct from one another, and I'm still convinced of it. Besides, I did my legal studies quite willingly and I believe they've also been useful to me. Perhaps one can grasp a certain legal cast of mind on my part from several features of my writing: I believe, for instance, that one can

glimpse a certain reasoning faculty in my poems, a sense of law. On the other hand, my earliest writings, in which I saw myself more clearly, date from the time when I began working. I had already written *Gesta Romanorum*, but it's from that point on that I began to write the things that for me are more important, even if always concealed, because there's experience there of the world of work or of the city, settings in which I'm a figure in the background, a witness, a spectator.

At this point, to the friendship with Sereni is added another very important friendship, with Carlo Betocchi. I met him on the occasion of a poetry prize that was called "Encounters with Youth": my mother was still alive, this had to be the year my father died, 1952, or the year after. This prize had a strong official character—I remember that De Gasperi was at the award ceremony—and it took some notice of all the branches of the arts: there was a prize for music, a prize for painting, and the one for poetry. Having heard about this event, I decided to enter by sending *Gesta Romanorum*, or rather a version of *Gesta Romanorum* that I later lost and of which no trace remains, unless perhaps in the files of this contest. When I got the announcement of the ceremony, which said that I was on the shortlist of candidates for the prize, I went to Rome with my mother. Only when I got there did I find out that I was actually the winner. I remember that the jury included Ungaretti (as the chair), Betocchi, Leone Piccioni, Adriano Grande, and maybe Fallacara as well: it was a pretty catholic group all in all, but at the highest level.

How did things go and how did your relationship with Betocchi develop?
While there wasn't any follow-up with Ungaretti—though he'd paid many compliments, even publicly, to the collection that won the prize—Betocchi was very approachable in his encounters with me, and he invited me to go and meet with him in Florence. So, after we'd written to each other a few times, I started going to visit him regularly: I brought him my things, we discussed them and he gave me some advice. He was a truly extraordinary reader, I'd never met anyone who read with such generosity, with such keenness and composure: he didn't let anything go by. Betocchi had the capacity to comprehend what was different from himself. He had the intelligence to appreciate poets who were very different from one another—Zanzotto, me, and Bellezza, for example; Sereni wasn't like that, he was more inclined toward those who, I won't say those who resembled him, but those who weren't far from him, even though he was quite discerning as an editor: for example, he was thoroughly hammered for taking up Pasolini, whom he could barely stand, even from a literary point of view.

Let's talk about your discipleship, if one can call it that, in connection with Betocchi . . .

Betocchi not only encouraged me greatly in what I was writing at that time, he encouraged me above all to keep at it, to go forward. He wasn't flattering: he showed me that I had the capacity to write a little bit of everything, but that sometimes it was hardly clear who I was. According to him, there was some merit in *Gesta Romanorum*, but he still didn't consider it a book that was truly my own. In our dealings he had a reservation, in the sense that he recognized a certain skill on my part (he himself arranged the publication of my poems in a few journals), and yet he saw that I hadn't yet turned onto the right path. In fact, I found my way when I began to write from inside the world of work. I remember sending him an early group of poems from *The Unhealthiness of the Air* that talked about my experience, what I'd been doing, what I'd been seeing, in the world of the work, the economy, the reality of Milan: then he wrote to tell me that he was completely satisfied, that this was what he wanted from me. He himself sent a group of these poems to *Letteratura*, then on his own initiative he contacted the publisher Vanni Scheiwiller to get me to put together a book. Coming out with a collection from Vanni was very important to me, because it was the house that had published Erba, Risi, all the poets that I thought were the best and that, after Sereni, represented the continuation of Lombard poetry.

I remember that, a short time after Betocchi had contacted them to have me assemble a book, Vanni telephoned me, while I was away from home, and left me this very brief message: "I got the book and I'm doing it right away." Then, of course, years passed between that message and the book's publication, but, to tell the truth, I've never had a mania for publication, I knew that the book was there and the important thing was to do good work. So much time passed before the book came out that in the meantime I published another one, *This Is the Catalogue* (1961), which is chronologically my first book, even though the poems in *The Unhealthiness* are older. *The Catalogue*, which contains later poems, was issued by Lampugnani Nigri as a kind of keepsake for friends. He was a friend of mine from high school who in the meantime had become my new employer: I had left San Quirico for a textile group that had factories in Veneto. I was still dealing with legal issues, staying in Milan, though it often happened that I had to travel to the various factories. As I recall, this was a pleasant enough experience. Lampugnani Nigri had started his publishing career with me, then he went on to Sereni and others. He was the one who sponsored the fine journal *Questo e altro* (*This and More*), which was born out of his and my friendship with Sereni, and which then included on its editorial staff Isella, Niccolò Gallo, and Pampaloni, and later on Angelo Romanò. I was much more than a contributor to the journal, I was practically running it, I was the editor who put it together.

All the important writers of that period appeared in *Questo e altro*, and many foreign writers appeared there, thanks to Sereni's great curiosity about what was happening in Europe: we were involved with both prose and poetry and also fueled the critical debate.

There, in the critical notes section, I began to publish items on poetry, including Rebora: you could say that my career as a critic began there, since I'd only published one other item in *aut aut*. Then, after *Questo e altro* ended (it had lasted from 1961 to 1963), Mondadori's *Paragone Letteratura* (*Comparison: Literature*) was born, and I contributed to it. I'd also published some poems in *Questo e altro*, with a very nice note by Betocchi about the poems of *The Houses of the Vetra*.

How did that journal end?

Questo e altro ended, I wouldn't say with friction between Sereni and Lampugnani Nigri, but nonetheless with some displeasure on Vittorio's part. The publisher, who'd expected more at the outset, realized that the journal was important but there hadn't been the response that he'd hoped for, and then, since it was losing too much money, he decided not to continue and Sereni was a little upset about it. Then I remember that Alberto Mondadori invited us to his house on the Piazza della Repubblica and proposed continuing the work of *Questo e altro* with a Milanese edition of *Paragone*, which had been taken over by Mondadori. There was a Florentine edition, a Roman one, and that Milanese one. Sereni, Cesare Segre, and Maria Corti were all part of this one, along with me. The editor was Longhi, along with Anna Banti. Some disputes immediately arose, especially between the Florentine and Milanese editions, so much so that Sereni, in order to show some autonomy, sponsored an idea of mine to create a section of the journal to be called "Matters of Poetry." I was involved in it along with some others, including Majorino and Cesarano. This was an autonomous section that was done in Milan and that they tolerated in Florence: it didn't last long, however, also because there was the Saggiatore crisis. However, despite my being a leading representative of the Milan edition, I had good personal relationships with the contributors to the other editions, above all with Anna Banti, and later on I was even a contributor to *Paragone*.

Did you already know Anna Banti from before?

No, I got to know her then through the early meetings at *Paragone*, along with Roberto Longhi. We got along well and continued to collaborate, likewise when I later became the poetry critic for *Paragone*. After Longhi died, I was one of only a few who still went to meet with Banti, since there were those who found her unbearable. And yet she was always pleasant enough to me, even though she was a little terrifying: she was one of those literary grandees that there used to be at one time, who ruled by force of personality.

How would you evaluate your long critical involvement with the various journals you've mentioned?

The experience of writing for journals was very important for me, I really think I learned everything from that kind of work, so much so that I criticize younger colleagues, poets and critics, for not having gone through the experience of working on journals, for not having gone through that "hackwork." Someone who makes a living writing for newspapers isn't a critic, he's a journalist. I learned to be a critic by writing for free, with the advantage of being completely free, without making problems for myself of communication, of space, without worrying about keeping the customer satisfied. This is something that's totally missing in the two generations that come between my contemporaries and yours: I'm referring to the generation of Cucchi, of Viviani. These writers have never done the kind of work I was just talking about, because they've lived in a period of effervescence that has helped them a lot, in period in which people published poetry easily and just as easily became critics on *Tuttolibri or Unità*: so they haven't had the apprenticeship of writing literary essays for journals. I think that this generation of the seventies, that has had an extraordinarily easy access to the major publishers—from the viewpoint of publishing books of poetry—and to the weekly and daily press, is lacking not only a bit of experience but also a real critical sense. In fact, there isn't any journal with which this generation has had a connection, except *Niebo*, which wasn't a journal of criticism, however, but of trends. I'm convinced that it's not possible to form one without journals, so I think that *clanDestino*, *Atelier* and other journals I could mention are, all things considered, forming a generation of critics.

The encounter with the language of journalism, by which I mean learning to write according to journalistic standards, is definitely useful, but I personally believe that I would never have learned to be a newspaper critic without all the work that I had previously done on journals: basic instruments, I repeat, for forming a generation's critical sense.

The first half of the seventies was extremely important for my formation because, naturally, writing for *Questo e altro* or *Paragone* meant not only writing, but also being in contact with the intellects of that period. I remember that at the meetings of *Questo e altro*, which took place in Via San Gregorio,

Sereni was there but so were those who were passing through Milan, Siciliano, for example, or Bellocchio. In other words, they were gathering-places, and the same thing happened in Florence with *Paragone*. I remember that at the "plenary" meetings of that edition practically all of them were there: figures like Bassani, Testori, Bertolucci, Ferrata, Serge, Corti, Niccolò Gallo, and Garboli.

What was discussed at those meetings?
They talked about a little of everything: which authors to include, which new writers to take seriously . . .

When did you begin to be a critic professionally?
The step before that of making money as a critic came when I entered the world of publishing in a direct way. I'd begun to involve myself in matters of publishing with Lampugnani Nigri, while my main work was still the other, then at a certain point I grew tired of this double life, which was becoming exhausting, so I began to live on editorial and journalistic contributions. I became a consultant to Garzanti at the end of the sixties, beginning of the seventies, which are also the years when I began my biggest translation jobs—Proust, for example. The period when I worked organically for Garzanti goes from roughly 1971–72 until 1976, then this job also became somewhat tiring and, while keeping a relationship with Garzanti, I started working with Mondadori, and I became a consultant for them, in addition to having a contract for the Proust translation.

While I was at Garzanti I became involved with *Tuttolibri*, which was just getting started, and at that point I became a working critic, no longer for literary journals: I wrote an article every week. Little by little writing criticism became my main occupation; after *Tuttolibri* I was offered a position with *Messaggero*. For a few months at the beginning of the eighties, I worked at both, then *Messaggero* became the more important commitment, onto which was later grafted a contract with *Europeo* (this was roughly 1982–83). In that instance I also worked for both of them for a while, trying to diversify: I did mostly reviews for *Messaggero* and current events, commentary, and other kinds of articles for *Europeo*. Later came the offer to be the drama critic for the *Corriere*; I left *Messaggero* and kept working for a little while at *Europeo*, and then I ended my involvement with that weekly.

And the publishing work?
With publishing the business faded away little by little: after Garanti there was the Mondadori period, where I worked as a consultant; then, after Sereni died, the business was waning, even though I stayed on for a little while with

De Maria, with Forti. I had another working commitment with Guanda, from the end of the seventies to around '83–'84. With Guanda I was involved in planning the relaunch and overseeing the Phoenix Notebooks and, with some other friends, such as Franco Cordelli, other series of prose volumes. Then, after leaving Guanda, the only publishing activity I've been involved in was the supervision of the poetry series for Marsilio, in the nineties.

I'd like to go back to the fifties: after your father and mother died, you got married. What do you recall from that time?
I got married in 1958, when I had just started working with Lampugnani Nigri. I have happy memories of the early years of my marriage, with my little children: the first one arrived after a year, and the other two in intervals of a few years. My ex-wife, Bianca Bottero, with whom I remained on excellent terms, was an architect. The early years, then, were a good time: pleasant and intense years. The marriage lasted until 1970, with something of a crisis on my part and other romances. It's odd because when I got married I was convinced that I'd made the best move, that I'd planned my life the right way, but then, as might possibly be seen obliquely in a few of my pieces from that period, in the sixties there began a period of unrest . . .

One thinks of the section "The Impediment," of course (in Deceptive Cadence, *1975).*
Yes. In fact, I actually lived these romances as an "impediment," in the sense that they upset the pattern of life that I appeared to have chosen for myself. So there began a period of a double life, in the sense that I tried to keep my marriage, which I wanted very much to hold on to, on its feet, but with obvious problems and imbalances. Then there was another affair that brought me to a definitive break. I remember the first years after my separation from my children with some anguish. They were at a special age, because they weren't babies anymore, but children who needed to be given explanations, ones that were far from easy to give. Those first years were not easy, despite the great and extremely intelligent cooperation of my wife. Then I got married again, a few years later, to Serena Vitale, even though I'd begun living with her when I left my home: the fact is, when we got married was when the crisis in our relationship began. In fact, in 1981 I met Patrizia Valduga and a rather complicated affair began, seeing as how she was also married, she was living in Belluno and going to school in Venice, while I was living and working in Milan. On top of all that, Serena, at that point, was teaching in Naples. For all these reasons, that was a time of great dislocations for me.

When I left Serena, despite our not having any children, she didn't take it as well as my first wife, and our relationship didn't survive the separation. Then I went to live by myself, and not long after that Patrizia, who had problems with her husband, broke it off with him as well. Patrizia graduated late, because she'd done three years of medicine at Padua before switching to literature when she became aware that she wasn't going to be able to attend anatomy classes. We met at her initiative: she wrote me and called me—she'd gotten my number from Guanda Publishing—to tell me she wanted to give me one of her books, and that's how it happened. When the final blowup with her husband occurred, she came to Milan and we got together, and we still are: we've been together now for twenty years. It's my longest "marriage" (in fact we've never married, partly for good luck): I was with my first wife for thirteen years and with Serena for ten.

Tell me something about the three children you had with your first wife. Have you kept up good relationships with them?
Yes. Giulia is the youngest, in the middle is Pietro, and the oldest is Lazzaro, who got married about two years ago. I have a very good relationship with them: a little of the credit goes to my persistence, but most of it is owing to my first wife, with whom both Patrizia and I have an extremely friendly relationship. I do actually have a good relationship with my children, even though I feel that I've failed them, as can be seen from the poem "The War" (in *With Such Dear Blood*, 1988). Even though it seems to me that things haven't gone badly for them, it's obvious that a father ought to do more for his children. My whole life basically consists of trying to put together things that are hard to reconcile, I'm someone who goes out of his way to look for problems for himself.

Who knows, maybe this way of living has been good for your poetry . . .
That may be, I can't rule it out.

I recall that when I interviewed you once before, several years ago, you challenged Montale's affirmation of living at five percent, and you told me that in your opinion the main thing for a poet is to live.
Yes, I think this with some conviction. Clearly, I still believe that poetry is a substitute for something that is somehow lacking, but if it lacks everything the substitute becomes a bit stifling. In short, we ought to live at least at fifty percent . . . Probably a person always writes when moved by something that hasn't been fulfilled, or that's been fulfilled in a way that wasn't what had been expected, or, from a certain point forward, out of awareness of not having done what should have been done.

Do you think that your poetry has a lot of this feeling of failure?
Yes, pretty much, or at least: I don't know about the poetry, but it's certainly there in my life. I'm rather troubled by the feeling, more or less conscious, of not having done my duty completely. For example, I can't help fulfilling a commitment to work that I've taken on: this is probably a reflection, or a concealment, of the feeling of not having kept my commitments of an emotional-sentimental-existential nature. Based on this perception, at least in my work I try to do everything I can.

Do you think that this is to some extent the reflection of a religious upbringing? Was your family Catholic?
Yes, they were: my mother was observant and practicing, my father less so. I remember with some amusement that my father would go with my mother and me to Mass on Sunday, but then he stayed outside, smoking and waiting for us: this seemed like a completely normal thing to me. I don't think this was an aberration, it was fairly widespread in many families that were Catholic or in any case not atheists and freethinkers. It was also another way, one a little more extreme, of explaining the division that had come about in the church between men and women. Moreover, before the interruption caused by the war, I went to school at Gonzaga—that is, in a school run by a religious order. I remember that my confessor was Don Carlo Gnocchi, a remarkable personality and a man endowed with a definite charisma.

Psychologically, do you connect this upbringing, at least in part, with your troubled spirit, or not?
To be honest, I have some difficulty in deciding. The sense of duty and of obligations assumed is certainly something that my father strongly instilled in me, with a vaguely Protestant ethic, even though there was nothing Protestant about my family: moreover, the idea of work is a deeply felt value in Lombard culture. I myself am aware of having almost a veneration of work well done: working just to work makes no sense, but working to work well is something else. I believe that this attitude of mine has complicated my life at times, but I don't think I could have lived any other way. From this may come my obsession with going back over everything: for instance, I've never been able to collaborate, because I tend to redo everything afterwards. I've tried a couple of times to make use of someone, demonstrating how to get started on a translation, but the results have been disastrous, because I lost much more time going back over it and redoing it.

Apart from what you told me about your feeling of failing your children, is there anything, looking back, that gives you a feeling of regret or remorse? In your poetry, for example in Every Third Thought *(1993), there's the idea of having closed outstanding accounts with the past.*
Yes, I believe that this sense of failing, which at a certain point was focused on my relationship with my children, was somehow pre-existent. In fact, even before I was separated from them I had the totally irrational feeling of having missed some important appointment, with my parents, for example, with whom I had a very good relationship. Maybe the fact that my father and mother died so early made me unconsciously feel somewhat responsible, as though I'd been unable to hold on to them. Then this feeling of failure took hold more rationally in connection with my children, with whom I really was inadequate in fulfilling my responsibilities. But I believe that something had already taken shape, purely irrationally, before that.

So their deaths were something of a shock . . .
Yet not having had from a certain point on any actual religious practice—I stopped going to confession quite early, even though I've never gotten out of the habit of praying, as I think can be seen in my poetry—I believe I said my most ardent prayers as a boy and a little child. I would ask that no one else die before I did. I was terrified by the thought of being separated from the people who were dear to me, like my parents. After they died I felt guilty for having outlived them.

In some of your older poems you talk about a little sister, or am I mistaken?
The little sister who was never born is a childhood fantasy. Obviously my parents must have asked me if I'd like to have a sister. For a little while this figure of the sister never born was intertwined with the story of a sister of my father's that I never met (just as I didn't know either one of my grandfathers) and who died very young from the Spanish influenza during the First World War. This figure of my father's sister was probably mixed up with the idea that I could also have had a sister. In "For C., Dead in Childbirth at the Age of One Year and Eleven Months" (in *Deceptive Cadence*) the "sister / who died ten years ago" is Serena's sister, who also died young.

After "The Impediment," the other erotic uprising in your poetry occurs in Mortal Canzonettes *(1985). Considering that booklet now, after having published other important books, do you think that it sounded a wrong note, or not?*
No, I like that book; I also like it, obviously, for sentimental reasons.

I mean to say, have you ever had second thoughts about using such direct erotic language, so different from the more coded diction you'd employed up to then?
No, I haven't had second thoughts, it was quite liberating for me, and then it was a rather significant formal turning point. It's a book that still pleases me, made up of two very different parts because the "Mortal Canzonettes" were actually written later: the other part, "Lista di Spagna," is a sort of diary. A diary written at a time when it seemed that it all had to end. In fact, there was a brief period, after meeting Patrizia and the most tumultuous part of our history, when we decided, because of prior emotional commitments, not to continue our relationship. Then I went to Naples, by myself, and I wrote this diary there in one shot over just a few days, the more erotic part of the book and the first part to be written, which is called "Lista di Spagna": it was a way I wanted to capture something that I thought was finished; and yet I wrote it in the present tense. The section of "Mortal Canzonettes" was written later, when I was already with Patrizia, and I wrote it in one night, in Rome, at a house where we were guests, when we had just started living together. The whole thing was published a few years after I wrote it. I remember a story about the reactions to the erotic language of *Canzonettes*. It concerns Cesare Cavalleri, the editor of *Studi Cattolici*, whom I knew a long time ago, when I was the film critic for *Avvenire* (I did that for three years, before *Tuttolibri*, from mid-1970 to '73). We knew each other as colleagues, since he also wrote for that paper. Cavalleri reviewed *With Such Dear Blood* (1988), in which *Mortal Canzonettes* was collected: well, while he had very nice things to say about the rest of the book, he referred to those as poems that should not have been written, about a story, quote, that should not have been lived, unquote.

*Apropos of your love for Patrizia: especially in your next-to-last book (*Quare Tristis*, 1998), but also in* With Such Dear Blood*—in the poem "Pain," for example—you hint at a somewhat uneasy relationship with this personage of the companion . . .*
Yes, the principal uneasiness is mine, in that there's a great age difference between Patrizia and me, twenty-two years: she was a girl and I was a mature man, and this brought in the main component of my anxiety. Then, from a certain point of view, she's not an easy person: she has an interweaving of insecurities and hypersecurities in her way of being, which eventually lead to health problems. I've never known anyone who had such a potential pathophobia while staying very healthy, as indeed she has. In fact, one of the first things she talked to me about, when we met, was her dread of illnesses, in addition to a certain fear of being alone. However, after we started living together, she managed to overcome a few problems: she overcame them only gradually, things that had

seemed to be character issues, imaginary or psychological, that had become real health problems. So this cluster of things caused me some pain . . . And yet this relationship, which on the whole always keeps getting better, is one of the few things that satisfy me and that I haven't regretted. Patrizia has given a great deal to me, from every point of view: of course all of that isn't free.

Another biographical theme in your poetry is that of illness. I'm thinking of the "Sonnets of Illness and Convalescence" in Every Third Thought . . .

Yes, I had a heart attack out of the blue in 1987, when I was 55. That was a shock, in that I started to have doubts about my "omnipotence": before that I thought I could do everything, endure any stress, but then I started to realize that that wasn't the case. The fact is, the heart attack came at a moment of terrible fatigue from work. I remember that when I found myself in the hospital emergency room—in Germany, to boot—I thought of it basically as a moment when I could stop to catch my breath. In fact, it was the period when I had a contract with the *Messaggero* and one with *Europeo*, and I had to give each of them at least one article every week; I was in the middle of my Proust translation and I felt I wasn't keeping up with it, and I had other work besides. On top of that, Patrizia and I were very taken with the theater of [Tadeusz] Kantor and we followed him everywhere we could. It was purely to indulge this passion that we left for Germany, to see one of Kantor's presentations. I got up at four in the morning to finish an article for *Europeo*, at eight a.m. we went to the airport, and before we landed at Frankfurt I had a pain in my chest, not a severe one, but unusual. I arrived in Frankfurt, hoping to shake it, but I wound up in the hospital. Then I went back to Italy, checked into a hospital for a few days, and had a fairly long convalescence. At that point, most opportunely, the offer came from the *Corriere* to be their theater critic: this allowed me to cut back a little on my commitments. Besides, for one thing, I found following the theater entertaining, and for another, I found writing about the theater much less exhausting.

Then in 1990 I had to have a kidney removed because they'd found that I had an adenoma. I had to face a fairly serious operation followed by a rather long convalescence; this is the experience I refer to in the sonnets in the first part of *Every Third Thought*. Finally, I had a bypass. I'd gone to have some tests done: I had some problems with hypertension and hardening of the arteries that, in my case, didn't cause pain, but only gave me a feeling of terrible anxiety. I remember that at that time the least little thing was enough to give me a strong feeling of anguish and oppression. So I had some heart tests and they found that my arteries were ninety percent occluded.

Regarding the heart attack, is there any trace of it in your poetry?
There's something. The last part of "Evening Invocations" (in *With Such Dear Blood*) refers directly to that experience. I conceived the idea for it and wrote it in Germany, after the attack. I lived through that experience, however, with great serenity: I felt at that time the "sensation" of death accompanied by an extreme calm.

I remember that when I got to the hospital, the doctors, seeing that I was in the middle of a heart attack, put nitroglycerine in my mouth and told me not to move because the situation was pretty serious. Then I had the feeling that I might even die, but I remember having experienced a great serenity. That was a real turning point for me, and it was also an opportunity to take stock of my life: I had definitely made quite a few mistakes, but I had accomplished something of what I wanted to do.

In fact, there is a strong sense of reconciliation in your most recent poems, even in dealing with the deaths of your loved ones, as when you talk about the communion of the living and the dead . . .
Yes, this has become one of my principal subjects of reflection and I've become much more serene with regard to the past. In other words, previously it was lived the way we talked about it, but now I feel that if I've survived maybe they've survived as well; soon, however, it will be the same thing, there's a larger design to be seen . . . Surely in this sense the shock of my heart attack represented a turning point. The kidney operation, on the other hand, has taken on a different significance, in that it was the first time that I underwent a surgical procedure. It was performed in France; in fact, I'd personally decided to be operated on in Nice by a very capable surgeon; in those surroundings, quite picturesque to anyone used to Italian doctors, there was a feeling of a great international community. I recall that the anesthetist was Tunisian and the nurses were from various parts of the world.

In some of your work, especially in Deceptive Cadence, *there is the theme of social engagement: the death of Pinelli and the ensuing Calabresi affair. How did you experience these events? What does ideological passion mean to you, if in fact you subscribed to it, and what remains of it?*
Mine was more of a civic passion than an ideological one. In the sense that I was never ideologically committed to anything, and I wasn't even a militant leftist in the strict sense, even though I identified with their ideas. As for the events of 1968–69 and what came after—namely, the Piazza Fontana bombing—I experienced them with the emotional involvement of a citizen

and therefore with great indignation. Those were the years of my friendship with Giorgio Cesarano, who on the other hand had had a real political adventure, he was a battlefield warrior of the left. He had a tormented history behind him, because he was a militant Fascist as a boy, then he joined the Communist Party, which threw him out when they found out about his past, and then in the end he killed himself. I was always more removed from these things, but since he was my friend and I admired him as a poet, I followed these events with him to some degree. To tell the truth, I followed them, as it seems to me now, as something of a "tourist," but they aroused my interest; I went to demonstrations, and at one of them the police beat the shit out of me. Among other things, I was already a critic for *Avvenire*. I remember that a picture appeared in the supplement of the *Domenica del Corriere* of me smeared with blood after I'd been assaulted by the forces of law and order.

How did you reconcile these positions with those of a Catholic daily like Avvenire*?*
I have wonderful memories, right up to the end, of my relationship with *Avvenire*, because they were very tolerant. When I think back on the things I wrote for *Avvenire*, it gives me the shivers, and something of that nature might not even be possible nowadays. The end of this collaboration was traumatic, however. I was kind of tired, and this tiredness probably had been an unconscious weight. At that time I was at the Venice Film Festival and I wrote a positive piece about a movie called *The Devils*, which was quickly banned and condemned by the Catholics. With this incident my collaboration with *Avvenire* came to an end, but I recall that the business was wrapped up in a civil manner, all things considered. The editor, I think it was Narducci, wrote me a letter in which he said that the writers at *Avvenire* didn't share my position and that they were in conflict with the whole festival, precisely because it had hosted that film. It was automatic that, because I had spoken well of it, I had to go: so I sent the editor a letter in which I said that I didn't feel like keeping on with it any longer. In any event, the height of my commitment to the Left occurred from 1968 to 1970.

During the '90s, there was talk in the newspapers—and you responded with an article—about various intellectuals, including Eco and yourself, having signed a manifesto for Lotta Continua.
I recall that a professional man, who had agreed to manage the Lotta Continua newspaper, had been charged with a crime that seemed to us to be purely a crime of opinion. So we published what he had written and we supported him. It was obviously a self-implication of solidarity that had nothing to do with

the supporting arguments: ours was a purely formal gesture. Years after the fact the signers of that initiative have been asked how they could ever have written such crazy things against the State, and the signers have responded in very different ways. I believe that I'm the only one to have recalled the intent of that initiative.

So you never had any association with Lotta Continua?
No, I never had any relationship with Lotta Continua, and from the outset I've always been absolutely opposed to terrorism, in the most unambiguous manner. Then in the interim my awareness of actual socialism took root: these were the years when I was with Serena, who was a Russian literature scholar, and we went often to the Soviet Union. I quickly realized with great clarity what the actual situation was. So in the seventies my position was post-Twentieth Congress of the CPSU.

There's a text dealing with Pinelli where you have the ironic image of the arch-angel Calabresi: this obviously was a moment of anger . . .
Of course, it was very hard, living in those times, not to be outraged. On the other hand, I wrote that piece before Calabresi was killed. Killing struck me as a horrible thing, just as grievous when it was done by the Left.

Looking at the present, various intellectuals of your generation seem to be feeling a kind of disillusionment, of disenchantment over the end of an ideology that they had believed in. You, on the other hand, have taken a quite different position . . .
Yes, I've never believed in any ideology. Certainly, up to a certain point in time the existence of an alternative to capitalism—namely, the idea of revolution and a different world—held out a hope. But when I saw the real situation in the USSR, I gave up on that prospect.

In your most recent poems you return to a civic vein, but one that's less corrosive and negative, almost from a position of endurance.
In fact, though it seems ridiculous to say so, poetry is kind of an alternative.

Looking back over your life, have you ever had second thoughts about having devoted yourself exclusively to literature and poetry? I mean to say, have you ever thought: "Who knows how it would have turned out if I had pursued my profession and my life in a different way?"
Yes, I've thought about it a few times. I'm still convinced that the ideal is to have a space of total autonomy for poetry and literature: so, if I have a regret,

it's that I didn't continue with the profession that I had. It wouldn't have made me unhappy to be a magistrate, or to have a university career, though not specifically in the field of literature. It's not so much a regret, it's more the idea of a life that might have been simpler, with a more favorable subdivision of things. After all, interweaving poetry, criticism, and cultural organization is rather tiring.

Is it tiring or, more accurately, misguided, according to you?
Maybe it's conceptually misguided, it would need to have another status.

And yet for you poetry was a necessity . . .
Please, poetry is a great part of my life, but it's a mistake to be a poetry critic at the same time. In fact, a few years ago I spoke about just this conflict of interest. Yet it's hard to come up with solutions, the only way is not to do it, as a profession, neither as a scholar or a cultural journalist, much less as an associate of publishers. I've tried to cut back gradually, in the sense that, for example, I've stopped being a working critic of poetry, but there are no definitive solutions. What's to be done? If one lives off these things, the conflicts of interest are endless.

And yet does the final word on you as a poet seem to you to be a positive one? That is, have you done, as they say, what you had to do?
I think so, yes.

Notes to the Poems

GESTA ROMANORUM

The phrase, Latin for "Deeds of the Romans," is the title of a medieval collection of tales, didactic in intent, many of them drawn from Greek and Roman legends and history. The title applies only loosely to the compilation, and Raboni's appropriation of it intends no connection to the contents of that volume.

I have translated in its entirety the group of poems gathered under this title in Raboni's *Tutte le poesie (1951–1998)*, about which he writes: "These are what remain of my first collection of poems, which won a prize in a contest for unpublished work but which was never issued and, at a certain point, was lost. A few of its texts had appeared, in the meantime, in reviews or anthologies, others as an 'Appendix 1951–1954' in *The Houses of the Vetra*, and still others in a privately printed chapbook titled *Gesta Romanorum* (1967)."

MEDITATION IN THE GARDEN

After his arrest, Jesus is brought before Annas, the former high priest of Israel (John 18:13).

ROUND

In the game of "owl," players try to knock the caps off one another's heads.

AT TARBES

Tarbes is a town in Gascony, in southern France, near Lourdes.

THE HOUSES OF THE VETRA

The Piazza della Vetra in central Milan, which took its name from the canal that ran through it, was for centuries the site of executions—of heretics, suspected witches, and others, including, most notoriously, Guglielmo Piazza and Gian Giacomo Mora, tortured to death in 1630 after being falsely accused of spreading the plague. The case is discussed in *Storia della Colonna Infame*

(*History of the Column of Infamy*, 1842), a work by Alessandro Manzoni (1785–1873), published as an appendix to the revised edition of his great novel *I promessi sposi* (*The Betrothed*, 1827). In the early twentieth century the canal was polluted by local tanneries, and beginning in 1934 the area was cleared and houses demolished to make way for an open public space. In a 2003 interview, Raboni described it as "a place where I've never lived, where I almost never go. When they asked me why I chose *The Houses of the Vetra* as a title, I answered: it's Manzoni, and only Manzoni, and the *History of the Column of Infamy* and the plague as metaphor. . . . It's definitely not a work of personal recollections."

THE VICEROY'S REGRET

According to Rodolfo Zucco, in his annotations to Raboni's *Opera Poetica* (2006), the poem's speaker is most likely Herod Antipas.

PORTAL

The poem was inspired by the bronze relief panels attached to the doors of the Basilica of San Zeno in Verona, which is also traditionally believed to be the site of the wedding of Romeo and Juliet.

THE COLONIAL ERROR

Quoted from Andre Gide's journal entry of May 3, 1904, the last line means "It's good that they nailed him, so he'd stay up."

TO MY SON IN THE COUNTRY

The Edison was the electric power utility operating in northern Italy at that time.

The snail and the talking cricket are characters in Carlo Collodi's *Pinocchio*; the caterpillar appears in Lewis Carroll's *Alice in Wonderland*.

PARTS OF A REQUIEM

Moving

Gondrand is an international transport company based in Basel, Switzerland, with branches in many countries in Europe and Asia.

THE IMPEDIMENT

The epigraph is from Petrarch's *Canzionere*, or *Rime sparse*, originally called *Rerum vulgarium fragmenta*.

The Initials

The poem turns on the Italian bureaucratic custom of recording names with the surname followed by the given name.

INQUIRY

In a 2004 interview, Raboni spoke of his grandfather, who, shortly after the death of his wife in childbirth, had married her very young sister, as the inspiration for the poem: ". . . looking at a photograph of the family, I seemed to see in the pose (it was a photo where there were the two sisters, one married and one unmarried and young), I thought I caught looks. . . . The facts of the matter I do not know."

THE DEAD MAN'S ALIBI

On December 12, 1969, a bomb went off at the headquarters of the Banca Nazionale dell'Agricoltura in the Piazza Fontana in Milan, killing 17 people and injuring 88. On the night of the 15th, Giuseppe Pirelli, a railway worker and prominent anarchist, fell to his death from a fourth-floor window at police headquarters, where he had been detained and questioned for three days. At a hastily convened press conference, police superintendent Marcello Guida maintained that Pirelli's alibi was a lie and that he had committed suicide (Raboni has pointed out that *Guida* is an anagram of *Giuda* [Judas]). Pirelli was subsequently cleared, and one of the officers involved, Luigi Calabresi, was accused of murdering him, but the charges were dropped for lack of evidence. Calabresi was shot to death in the street on May 17, 1972, in retaliation. Pirelli's death was also the inspiration for Dario Fo's play *Morte accidentale di un anarchico* (1970).

THE GAME OF THE WORLD

"[T]he executed commissioner" is a reference to Luigi Calabresi (see note to "The Dead Man's Alibi" above).

FOR C., DEAD IN CHILDBIRTH AT THE AGE OF ONE YEAR AND ELEVEN MONTHS

C. was a pet cat called Caviale ("Caviar"). Elsa is the novelist Elsa Morante (1912–1985), a friend of Raboni and his wife.

INTERIORS: CLINIC

The poet Bartolo Cattafi died of cancer at age 56 on March 13, 1979. Raboni co-edited his *Poesie 1943–1979* (1990).

LISTA DI SPAGNA

"*Lista* was the strip of land in the neighborhood of embassies; this one was called Spanish from the old location of the embassy in the nearby palazzo that once belonged to the Zeno family": G. Lorenzetti, *Venice and Its Estuary* (as cited by G.R.).

The epigraph is from an aria in Lorenzo Da Ponte's libretto for Mozart's *Don Giovanni*, in which Leporello is enumerating his master Don Giovanni's sexual conquests, including, among others, one thousand and three in Spain, six hundred and forty in Italy, and ninety-one in Turkey (cf. the section of the poem beginning "No, I haven't had a thousand and three").

"Titian's / banners at the Frari": the reference is to the painting known as the *Madonna di Ca' Pesaro* (1519–1526) in the Basilica di Santa Maria Gloriosa dei Frari in Venice.

Veronica Lake: American film actress (1922–1973), best known for Preston Sturges' *Sullivan's Travels* (1941) and René Clair's *I Married a Witch* (1942).

"Strings, a flute . . . ," etc., is the orchestration for the aria *Dalla sua pace* (*Don Giovanni*, Act One, Scene XIV), in which Don Ottavio speaks of his love for Donna Anna.

"*Les feux d'une rousse chevelure*" ("The flames of a head of red hair") is from *À l'ombre des jeunes filles en fleurs* (*In the Shadow of Young Girls in Flower*, known more familiarly in English as *Within a Budding Grove*, 1919), the second volume of Marcel Proust's *À la recherche du temps perdu*.

"Some the folia, some the allemande . . .": quoted from an aria by the title character in *Don Giovanni*, Act One, Scene XV. The folia is a musical theme, the allemande an instrumental dance, both of sixteenth-century origin.

"*Blanche fille aux cheveux roux*" ("Pale girl with red hair") is the opening line of *À une mendiante rousse* ("To a Redhaired Beggar"), poem LXXXVIII of Charles Baudelaire's *Les Fleurs du mal.*

LANDING

Salute and San Tomà are two of the points at which ferries cross the Grand Canal in Venice.

The imagery of the poem evokes the description of the souls of the dead waiting to be ferried by Charon across the Acheron in Canto III of Dante's *Inferno*.

EVENING INVOCATIONS

The term *monatto* refers to someone who collects and buries the dead during a plague.

CONVERSATION ABOUT NOTHING

In a candle auction, bidding ends when the candle (or candles) burns down and goes out. The inability to predict when that moment will occur is intended to prevent last-second bids.

INTERIOR EXTERIOR

Tressette ("three sevens") is a popular card game.

The antecedents of the pronouns in the last two lines are "armchair" (line 1) and "embers" (line 4).

THE FAREWELLS

"*[L]a servante au grand coeur*" ("The great-hearted servant") is the beginning of poem C of *Les Fleurs du mal.*

"FOR AN UNFORESEEN REASON . . ."

The action takes place on Monday, June 10, 1940, the date on which Mussolini declared war on France and Britain (obliquely touched upon in the reference to the radio in the last sentence).

The comments on the theater façade and the disappearance of the plane trees allude to the effects of the Allied bombing of Milan in August 1943.

"[F]our years, ten months and fifteen days" looks forward to April 25, 1945, the date of the liberation of Turin and Milan; since 1949, April 25 has been an official national holiday in Italy known as Liberation Day.

"Forty-four years, one month and one day" carries the action forward to July 11, 1984, the presumptive date of the text's composition.

SONNETS OF ILLNESS AND CONVALESCENCE

This group of poems grew out of a kidney operation and extended hospital stay that Raboni underwent in 1990. Several similar examples may be familiar to English-language readers, including W. E. Henley's "In Hospital" (*A Book of Verses*, 1888), an untitled sequence by Richard Blessing (*Poems & Stories*, 1983), and Vernon Scannell's "The Year of the Crab" (*Of Love and War*, 2002).

"No lack of void . . ."

The opening phrase is quoted from a speech of Estragon's in Samuel Beckett's *Waiting for Godot*.

"Morning swarmed . . ."

sine macula: Latin for "without stain"

with drums and colours: an allusion to the endings of a number of Shakespeare's plays.

"'FALLEN IN AFRICA,' SURE, WHY WOULDN'T HE BE?"

According to Raboni, the quoted phrase was taken from a roadside plaque. "A.O." stands for *Africa Orientale* (East Africa) and refers to Mussolini's invasion of Ethiopia in 1935–36.

Patmos is a Greek island; the Book of Revelation is traditionally ascribed to John of Patmos, who may or may not have been the evangelist.

"BETWEEN THE ANSCHLUSS AND THE KRISTALLNACHT"

The Anschluss, Hitler's annexation of Austria, occurred on March 12, 1938.

Kristallnacht, the "night of broken glass," a pogrom against Jewish property and lives throughout Germany, took place on November 9–10, 1938.

The Munich Agreement, ceding parts of Czechoslovakia to Nazi Germany, was signed on September 30, 1938.

The German attack on Danzig, Poland, on September 1, 1939, was the start of the Second World War.

In Greek mythology, Charon is the ferryman who conveys souls across the Styx and Acheron rivers to the world of the dead.

STANZAS FOR THE MUSIC OF ADRIANO GUARNIERI

Adriano Guarnieri (b. 1947) is an Italian composer of classical music. *Quare tristis*, his setting of Raboni's poem for soloists, chorus, two instrumental groups, and live electronics, was premiered at the Venice Biennale in 1995.

Quare tristis es anima mea? (Latin: "Why art thou sad, O my soul?") is from Psalm 42.

[U]t nobis Corpus et Sanguis fiat ("That it may become for us the Body and Blood" of Christ) is from the Canon, or Eucharistic Prayer, of the traditional Roman Catholic Mass.

In addition to the citation of the song "Full fathom five thy father lies" from Shakespeare's *Tempest* in lines 34–35, Rodolfo Zucco points out several echoes in Raboni's poem of "The Caged Skylark" by Gerard Manley Hopkins and "A Song for Simeon" by T. S. Eliot.

"THE POPLARS—WHAT POSSIBLE SIGNIFICANCE"

See the note to "For an unforeseen reason . . ." above.

"YOU'LL WALK ON WATER SO THAT YOU CAN GO"

"Saint John, chapter 20, verse 16": "Jesus saith unto her, Mary. She turned herself, and saith unto him, Rabboni; which is to say, Master" (KJV). Rodolfo

Zucco, however, cites the explanation in Emidio De Felice's *Dizionario dei cognomi italiani* (1978) that the name Raboni derives from an elision of the phrase *ora buòna* ("good hour," or "propitious time").

"THEN THE WORLD'S BORDERS AREN'T SO UNCLEAR"

Benito Mussolini, his mistress Clara Petacci, and several others were shot and killed by partisans on April 28, 1945; the next day, their bodies were hung upside down from a gas station roof in the Piazzale Loreto in Milan.

"I, THEIR GUEST, OR THEY MINE IN THE ENCHANTED"

in articulo vitae: Latin for "at the point of life," a play on the common phrase *in articulo mortis*.

"I DON'T KNOW, NO, I DON'T KNOW YET, I'D GUESS"

Mario Sironi (1885–1961) was an Italian painter whose work passed through phases of Cubism and Surrealism but became increasingly realistic in the 1920s.

"IN THE TIME, NOW, OF ASHES, JUST A FEW"

The "avenue" is the Corso Buenos Aires in northeastern Milan, the city's main shopping street. In this area there was built, from 1489 to 1509, the Lazzaretto, or leprosarium, of Milan, a square, walled enclosure measuring some 1200 feet on each side. In its center stood a small temple that was replaced in 1589 by an octagonal church, which still stands. Milan was struck by major outbreaks of plague in 1524, 1576, and 1629, the last of which is vividly described in Manzoni's *I promessi sposi*. After this last plague, the Lazzaretto was put to other uses, mostly military, until it was bought by the Banca di Credito Italiano in 1881 and demolished over the following decade; a neighborhood of planned streets and buildings was constructed in its place. In 1884 the church was dedicated to Saint Charles Borromeo (1538–1584), who had been the archbishop of Milan during the plague of 1576 and the ensuing famine brought on by a crop failure, and who ministered to the victims of these disasters, tending to the sick and feeding the hungry, exhausting his personal fortune in the process.

Malebolge ("Evil Ditches") is the eighth circle of hell in Dante's *Inferno*, described in Cantos XVIII–XXX. It is made up of ten concentric circular ditches, each called a *bolgia*; each houses a separate category of sinners.

Parini and Carducci are Milanese high schools attended by Raboni in the 1940s. They are named for the Italian poets Giuseppe Parini (1729–1799) and Giosuè Carducci (1835–1907).

AM-lira (Allied Military lira) was currency printed in the United States and put into circulation in Italy by the Allied occupation between July 1943 and April 1945; it continued to be legal tender in Italy until June 1950.

"THE TUGBOAT PASSING BY"

The poem was inspired by Raboni's visit to the United States in April 2001. The details of the description have led Alfredo de Palchi to believe that the setting is Philadelphia and the Delaware River.

"THERE WERE, IN THE YEAR OF 1943"

Como is a city and Luino a town in northernmost Italy, on the Swiss border. The implication is that the Russian émigré smuggles people into Switzerland.

Mischa Auer (1905–1967) was a Russian-born Hollywood actor best known for his roles in such comedies as *My Man Godfrey* (1936) and *You Can't Take It with You* (1938).

Achille Beltrame (1871–1945) was an Italian artist who illustrated the front and back covers of every issue of the Sunday supplement of the Milan daily the *Corriere della Sera* from the magazine's founding in 1899 until two weeks before his death forty-six years later.

"THEY BEAT HIM BLOODY, ALTHOUGH NOT TO DEATH"

"Giovinezza" ("Youth") was the official anthem of the Fascist Party and the Italian Army under Mussolini. It was also the official anthem of the Italian Social Republic, the Nazi puppet state headed by Mussolini and officially dissolved on April 25, 1945 (see note to "For an unforeseen reason . . ." above).

Masnago is a *frazione*, or ward, of the city of Varese in northernmost Italy; Induno Olona is a town in the province of Varese.

"I REMEMBER TOO MANY THINGS ABOUT ITALY"

Pier Paolo Pasolini (1922–1975), the noted Italian poet, novelist, and filmmaker, was, in his own individualistic manner, a committed leftist.

"[T]he miracle" is a term often applied to a period of sustained economic growth in Italy in the 1950s and early 1960s.

Paolo Volponi (1924–1994) was an Italian poet and novelist; he was elected to the Senate as a Communist in 1983 and held office until 1994.

The Italian general election of March 27, 1994, brought about a huge defeat for the leftist establishment in the wake of financial scandals and victory for the coalition led by Silvio Berlusconi, resulting in his first appointment as prime minister.

ON WATER

Sull'acqua was a limited-edition artist's book containing uncollected poems by Raboni and collages by the Italian artist Enrico Baj (1924–2003).

SONG OF THE NEW ERA

Introduced in 1927, the Fascist calendar counted the beginning of the Fascist era as October 29, 1922, the day after Mussolini was handed the reins of government, and marked the years of the regime, which lasted roughly twenty years, with Roman numerals. This system of dating was adopted by Ezra Pound, who was resident in Italy during this time and an ardent supporter of Mussolini.

Berlusconi's first electoral victory came in March 1994, but his tenure in office lasted less than a year; his last electoral victory (at the time of the poem's composition) occurred in May 2001.

Propaganda Due (P2) was a secret Italian Masonic lodge that had among its members a number of prominent business, military, and political figures, including Berlusconi. Bent on making the Italian government more right-wing and authoritarian, it was implicated in several scandals involving bribery, financial manipulations, and even murder. Its charter was withdrawn in 1976. (Interestingly, by a bit of stretch the phrase *ingresso nella loggia* could also yield the meaning "entrance onto the balcony," with its evocation of Mussolini.)

Channel 5 is a national television channel, one of three (out of seven national channels) owned by Fininvest, a financial holding company controlled by the Berlusconi family. With a schedule of American and domestic dramas, talk shows, variety shows, and reality shows, it is notorious for the vapidity and vulgarity of its programming.

TEMPUS TACENDI

The title, from Ecclesiastes 3:7, is Latin for "a time to be silent."

"I FEEL AS IF I'M LIVING IN A VACUUM"

Paolo is Paolo Volponi (see note to "I remember too many things about Italy" above).

A psychomachy (or psychomachia) is a spiritual conflict. The term derives from the *Psychomachia* (c. 400) of Prudentius (348–c. 413), a Latin allegorical poem of nearly a thousand lines in which virtues and vices battle one another.

THE SQUARE

Flanér: French for "to loll, to stroll, to saunter, to loaf."

Turmac (for Turkish Macedonian Tobacco Company) was a brand of cigarettes manufactured from 1920 to 1960, noted for their gold-colored mouthpieces and decorative packages.

PRIVATE PRAYER

John 20:16: see note to "You'll walk on water so that you can go" above.

"YOU HAVE TO REALIZE, CHRIST DIDN"T LOVE"

"(John, chapter 8, verse 6)":
"3 And the scribes and Pharisees brought unto him a woman taken in adultery; and when they had set her in the midst,
4 They say unto him, Master, this woman was taken in adultery, in the very act.
5 Now Moses in the law commanded us, that such should be stoned: but what sayest thou?

6 This they said, tempting him, that they might have to accuse him. But Jesus stooped down, and with his finger wrote on the ground, as though he heard them not.
7 So when they continued asking him, he lifted up himself, and said unto them, He that is without sin among you, let him first cast a stone at her.
8 And again he stooped down, and wrote on the ground." (KJV)

According to the *New York Times* of May 15, 1985, on the previous day, in "a speech before one of the smallest crowds ever seen on a papal trip, the Pope [John Paul II] told several hundred young people at an outdoor meeting" in Amersfoort, the Netherlands, that "[t]he church's teachings on 'marital love, abortion, sexual relations before or outside marriage or homosexual relations . . . remain the standard for the church for all time.'"

John Paul II was an avid skier.

"EVENING OF JANUARY 27, 1897"

This is essentially a found poem, assembled from several passages of a text in the first volume of *Le faville del maglio* ("Sparks from the Hammer," 1924), a compilation of essays, articles, journal entries, and other writings by Gabriele d'Annunzio (1863–1938).

"THE APULIAN GREENGROCER"

Clemente Rebora (1885–1957) was a Milanese poet who entered a seminary in 1930 and was ordained into the priesthood six years later.

"SO THEN, IS IT POSSIBLE FOR A MAN TO BE"

On July 22, 2003, acting on an informant's tip, U.S. forces stormed a villa in Mosul, Iraq, and engaged in a six-hour firefight with its occupants, killing Saddam's sons Uday and Qusay Hussein, their bodyguard, and Qusay's fourteen-year-old son.

[A]d personam is a Latin phrase, usually employed in a legal context, meaning "at or to a particular person."

Acknowledgments

My text for all of Raboni's poetry published in book form before *Barlumi di storia* is *Tutte le poesie (1951–1998)*; although the titles of the sections, the groupings of the poems, and the texts themselves sometimes vary from their original publications, I have preferred this edition because it is the last one overseen by Raboni and thus represents his final choices and judgments. The selections from *Barlumi di storia* and *Ultimi versi* have been taken from the original editions of those volumes, and the selections from *Sull'acqua* and *Versi dispersi e d'occasione* as they appear in *L'opera poetica*, edited by Rodolfo Zucco, whose superb annotations to this definitive collection of Raboni's poetry have been of invaluable assistance to me in compiling the notes to the poems.

Patrizia Valduga's essay was the introduction to *Nell'ora della cenere*, a selection of Raboni's poetry published by the *Corriere della sera* in 2012. Raboni's remarks on "The Wedding" were published by Liguori Editore in 1986 in *Il poeta e la poesia*, edited by Nicola Merola. Daniele Piccini's interview with Raboni appeared in the January 2003 issue of the magazine *Poesia*, published by Nicola Crocetti. I am grateful to the copyright holders of these materials for permission to translate them.

A number of these translations, sometimes in slightly different versions, appeared in the following journals: *Able Muse*: "Between the Anschluss and the Kristallnacht," "I'm what you were, it won't be long before," "The house out in the country where I'd stay"; *American Poet*: "Chorus," "Requiem for a Birthday"; *Café Review*: "For C., Dead in Childbirth at the Age of One Year and Eleven Months," "The Dead Man's Alibi"; *Chelsea*: "Codicils," "Lista di Spagna," "Mortal Canzonettes," "The Wedding"; *Evansville Review*: "The poplars—what possible significance"; *Gradiva*: "The Apartment," "I remember too many things about Italy"; *Iambs & Trochees*: "Is it so hard to imagine paradise," "There are evenings when I wish I could look out"; *Journal of Italian Translation*: "The aging body wants a different soul," "At times in autumn there are lights so clear," "The Farewells," "Lessons of Political Economy," "Little Boy Dead from Struggling Etc.," "Little Person," "My bad, my good, by now so close that I," "Renewal," "There was never a time when I was twice your age," "They beat him bloody, although not to death," "To go away, to come back home again"; *Raintown Review*: "No hopes and no desires: I'd have said." I am very grateful to the editors of these journals—especially to

Luigi Bonaffini and Luigi Fontanella, who helped with a number of difficult passages—for their receptiveness to my work.

"Movie Theater in the Afternoon" and "There are evenings when I wish I could look out" appeared in *The FSG Book of Twentieth-Century Italian Poetry*, edited by Geoffrey Brock.

"The poplars—what possible significance" was the co-winner of the Willis Barnstone Translation Prize for 2008. I extend heartfelt thanks to Willis Barnstone and everyone connected with the award, and to Maria Terrone for suggesting that I enter the competition.

I am once again grateful to everyone at Chelsea Editions for all their excellent work in bringing this book to such a satisfying realization. Alfredo de Palchi began the process by telling me of Giovanni Raboni's interest in having me translate his poetry and by encouraging me to undertake the assignment, and he remained steadfast in support of it throughout the seemingly endless process of its completion. Ned Condini (esteemed poet and translator and friend of many years' standing who, sadly, died before the book went to press) provided a thorough reading of both the Italian and English texts, catching many mistranscriptions and offering a number of clarifications. Lisa Cicchetti created the striking design of both the cover and the text, and Areta Buk performed a masterful job of typesetting.

In the early stages of this project, I was extremely fortunate to win the Raiziss/de Palchi Translation Fellowship. I am enduringly grateful to the Sonia Raiziss-Giop Foundation for both the generous cash prize and the opportunity to spend a magnificent month at the American Academy in Rome. I fondly recall the glorious milieu of the Academy and the generous spirit of everyone there, along with the unparalleled opportunity to explore one of the world's most fascinating cities.

It is with fond memories and great pleasure that I acknowledge the great assistance given me by my friend and colleague, the translator and novelist Gayle Ridinger, during my visit to Milan. She and her family graciously provided me the hospitality of their home, and she showed me around the city, arranged my meeting with Giovanni Raboni, and made it possible for him and me to communicate fluently with one another.

I owe a great debt to Patrizia Valduga, who, in my frequent communications with her, was a model of both tact and helpfulness. Never once did she comment on my choice of poems for the volume, either to commend or to criticize; never did she suggest the inclusion or the omission of any text; on the other hand, she graciously allowed me to overrule her initial hesitation and include here her introduction to her edition of Raboni's selected poems.

She also suggested the title of this volume, which is that of Raboni's 1993 collection. Most significantly, after I had completed the initial draft of the translation, she expended a great deal of time and effort to provide me with her own English version of virtually every poem in my selection. Her translations resolved a number of difficult passages and made me aware of further subtleties and depths in many of Raboni's works. There is hardly a poem in this volume that has not benefited from her involvement, which has helped to make it a better book than it would otherwise have been.

—Michael Palma

About the Author

GIOVANNI RABONI was born on January 22, 1932, in Milan, where he lived his entire life except for a period of relocation during the Second World War. Trained as a lawyer, he worked as a young man in the legal departments of several corporations, but thereafter earned his living principally as an editor and critic. His many volumes of poetry were collected in *Tutte le poesie (1951–1998)*, which was followed by *Barlumi di storia* (2002) and the posthumous *Ultimi versi* (2006). His status as perhaps the greatest Italian poet of his generation is attested to by the inclusion of his complete poems, *L'opera poetica* (2006), in the prestigious Meridiani series of standard Italian authors. He also published several volumes of critical essays, as well translations of Baudelaire's *Les Fleurs du Mal* and Proust's *A la recherche du temps perdu*, among many others. He died in Parma on September 16, 2004.

Much more information, along with many photographs and other supplementary material, can be found at http://www.giovanniraboni.it.

About the Translator

MICHAEL PALMA's poetry collections are *The Egg Shape*, *Antibodies*, *A Fortune in Gold*, and *Begin in Gladness*, and an Internet chapbook, *The Ghost of Congress Street: Selected Poems*, on The New Formalist Press website. His thirteen previous translations of modern Italian poets include prize-winning volumes of Guido Gozzano and Diego Valeri with Princeton University Press, as well as Maurizio Cucchi's *No Part to Play: Selected Poems 1965–2009* (Chelsea Editions, 2013). His fully rhymed translation of Dante's *Inferno* was published by Norton in 2002 and reissued as a Norton Critical Edition in 2007.